FACING THE RISING SUN

Oronde A. Miller

FACING THE RISING SUN

Perspectives on African American Family and Child Well-Being

Oronde A. Miller

Institute for Family and Child Well-Being
Bowie, MD

Published by The Institute for Family and Child Well-Being
Bowie, Maryland
http://www.ifcwb.org

Library of Congress Control Number: 2009932266
ISBN 978-0-9824840-1-2

First U.S. Edition
September 2010

Printed in the United States of America

Editorial Assistance: Karen Butler, Jaiya John, Khari Miller
Cover Design, Cover Photograph, Book Layout: Oronde A. Miller

This book is dedicated to...

...my daughter, **Aya Nyela**, and my son, **Damani Askia**. You are a bright shining light. Every day you help me to better understand and appreciate that life truly is a continuous *process of becoming and re-becoming*. You carry within your soul the wisdom of the Creator and our Ancestors. Go forth and share your message with the world, as we continue to reclaim *Our Way*.

...my brother, **Khari Askia Miller**. You've been with me since the beginning. As we both know, that's not to be taken for granted. I admire and appreciate your example of courage and determination, so many times in the presence of tremendous adversity and challenge. You possess an inspiring *warrior spirit* that demonstrates the capacity for individuals to learn, transform and *re-become*. I always find inspiration in your story.

...my parents **Georgella and Ellword Miller**. If my single contribution in this life is to be nearly as great a parent to your wonderful grandchildren as you have been to Khari and me, then my greatest potential accomplishment in this life will have been achieved. Thank you for your example of how to live a life of service, personally and professionally, in support and protection of our community's most valuable resource… our children.

...the founding executive director of Homes for Black Children in Detroit, Michigan, **Ms. Sydney Duncan**. It was your compassionate spirit and courageous leadership while developing and guiding this nation's first African American adoption agency that made our family possible. I will forever be grateful for your role in providing Khari and me with the priceless gift of a family.

...our **Ancestors**, and the countless generations of **children and families** whose voices have never been heard, and whose stories have never been told.

In appreciation of...

The Creator, Giver and Sustainer of All Life, and The Ancestors.

My lifelong circle of support and encouragement: Georgella and Ellword Miller, Khari Miller, and the Extended Family. Aya Nyela and Damani Askia for your encouragement to hurry up and finish. Amina Watson, for your understanding and support, especially during these final stages. Delores and Elbert Nance, Christopher Brigmon, Kevin Gibson, Brett Allen, Yohance Maqubela, and Jaiya John for your consistent encouragement and guidance through this process.

The early professional path... The National Center Staff: Jaiya John, Jacquelyn Bailey Kidd, James Craigen and Rebecca Jones Gaston, Tara Patterson. The Advisory Council: Sydney Duncan, Robert Hill, Ruth McRoy, J. Toni Oliver, Walter Perkins, Joseph Crumbley, Ruth Amerson, Zena Oglesby, Cynthia Willard, Linda West, Linda Whitfield, Annie Brown, Clarice Walker, Mae Best, O. Delmar Weathers, Sandy Lawrence, Wendy Lewis Jackson, C. Lynne Edwards. The Illinois Steering Committee: Annetta Wilson, Mike Burns, Cretora Barnett, Marcia Williams, Addie Hudson, Terry Solomon, Frances Elbert, Debra Dyer-Walker.

The Elders, Pioneers, Friends & Colleagues: Carol Spigner, Jestina Richardson, Rev. Richard Richardson, Andrew Billingsley, Jeanne Giovannoni, Sandra Jackson, Sharon Lowe, Erwin McEwen, Dorothy Roberts, William Thorne, Millicent Williams, Joyce James, Heidi McIntosh, Siobhan Trotman, Leonard Dunston, G. Rosaline Preudhomme, Joe Kroll, Ernestine Jones, Anna McPhatter, Laura House, Kikora Dorsey, Jackie Contreras, Anita Shannon, Cheryl Blanchette, Kary James, Madge Haynes, Ginger Pryor, Yakiciwey Washington Mitchell, Bernard Caliman, Anthony Williams, Russell Woods, Carlette Randall, Carolyne Rodriguez, Constance Rice, Gloria Burgess, Leonard Burton, Ernie Cathcart, Jorge Cabrera, Kristin Ward, Donna Parish, Brendan Hargett, Pamela Watkins, William Bell, David Sanders, The extended circle of friends and colleagues from Casey Family Programs, Participants and Faculty from the CFP Disproportionality Breakthrough Series Collaborative, Ruth White, Ada White, Friends and colleagues from The Child Welfare League of America, The courageous CCC judges of the National Council of Juvenile and Family Court Judges, Brenda Donald for bringing me into public child welfare, and the many other individuals not mentioned by name, but who have shaped my thinking about this critically important work.

A special thanks to Karen Butler for squeezing in time and tapping those earlier journalism skills to provide editorial assistance on the final manuscript.

CONTENTS

Preface

The essays compiled in this book are born most immediately out of my desire to make sense of the experiences of African American children and families caught in the web of this nation's child welfare and juvenile justice systems, and the experiences of professionals in various institutions and systems that work with and on their behalf.

In writing these essays, and thus in making them available in book form, I am clear that any successful effort by African Americans to reclaim and protect our children and families must begin with an acknowledgement that *ideas matter.* In order for anyone interested in supporting the healing and development of African American families and communities, we must first acknowledge and then change *how and what we think* about African American families and communities. I am clear about the power of ideas, and hope that in reading this book you also further appreciate this importance. As we clarify our ideas, our practice and our personal commitment will naturally respond to this shift. This applies to African Americans as well as others genuinely concerned about and committed to the healing and development of African American families and communities.

Facing the Rising Sun is about the ideas and values that govern our work with and on behalf of African American children and families. It's my attempt to articulate a set of ideas based upon a set of values and assumptions about what is good for children, families and communities, as well as a set of observations about the ways in which systems and institutions try hard yet come up short in supporting the real needs of families and communities. This book does not pretend to provide a set of "ultimate" answers, magic wand solutions or five-point plans. I believe the answers exist within the various communities around this country. My hope is that the ideas shared within this book help those of you who are genuinely concerned about African American children, families and communities assess and reassess your own assumptions and judgments about the challenges we continue to struggle through and against every day.

Facing the Rising Sun may appear to be relevant only to individuals somehow connected to this nation's child welfare or juvenile justice systems. Upon reading, however, one may quickly realize that the messages in this book are much broader in scope, its relevance and implication. This book can most appropriately be considered a meditation on the integrity of the African American experience in this country, and the ways in which systems influence that experience.

It's about the responsibility we all share to care for and support one another, thus creating families and communities in which all of our children thrive. It's about the responsibility we all share to create a safety net within our communities so that children and families, when struggling, can get the kinds of support they need, thereby minimizing the need for punitive human service and juvenile justice system involvement. It's also about the ways in which this nation's human and social service systems could be transformed *from* systems that assess for individual pathology and that ration supports and services to those considered most cooperative and deserving, *into* systems that proactively identify fundamental needs and support the healing and development of human beings and family systems in ways that are culturally affirming and integrity-based.

What about the title and cover?

In 1972, Andrew Billingsley and Jeanne M. Giovannoni published a book entitled *Children of the Storm: Black Children and American Child Welfare*. In my opinion this book stands as the most thorough analysis and survey of the African American experience with this nation's child welfare system to date (*Shattered Bonds*, a more recent contribution by Dorothy Roberts adds great and updated richness and texture to this story). I became aware of Billingsley and Giovannoni's work during my early years working in the field of child welfare.

In most discussions about the plight of African American children in this nation's child welfare system I hear little to no mention of this critically important work, yet almost four decades later it remains equally as relevant in its analysis. I implore everyone to revisit *Children of the Storm* as a critical step in reorienting ourselves to the experiences of African American children and families with this nation's child welfare system.

The African American experience in this country, especially our involvement with this nation's child welfare, juvenile justice, and other punitive and punishment-oriented systems, is indeed appropriately characterized as a storm. This storm experience has severely disrupted the cultural fabric of our community, especially the socialization experiences of our children and the fabric of relationships within our families and communities. This very storm experience has always, however, been met with resistance and a fundamental commitment among African American families to persevere and restore our community's way.

This enduring spirit of resistance and commitment is most eloquently captured in the poem of James Weldon Johnson, *Lift Every Voice and Sing.* This poem, said to have first been performed in February of 1900, would be put to music five years later by James Weldon Johnson's brother, John Johnson, and has for many generations now been recognized as the Black National Anthem. In this poem, James Weldon Johnson implores us to raise our voices to the skies, tell the story of African people in this country and throughout the diaspora, and (informed by our faith, wisdom and hope) continue on the path of our God, our ancestors and our native land. This book's title was inspired by the closing lines of the poem's first verse, *"Facing the rising sun, of our new day begun, let us march on, 'till victory is won!"*

Facing the Rising Sun is offered as a reminder that after every stormy night or season comes a beautiful and life-sustaining sunrise. Our individual and collective responsibility is first and foremost to be *mindful* (in the truest sense of this word) of the sunrise, its healing properties and potential, and the reminder it represents that a new day is beginning. My personal prayer and meditation is that from this day forward, every rising sun reveals a community of families, professionals and organizations standing with renewed clarity of purpose and courage, and a fundamental commitment to the healing and development of African American families and communities.

An Adinkra Values Framework

During my years in college and graduate school, I wondered why so few of our professors ever discussed the concepts and theories of child development and socialization developed by African people over the centuries. I was becoming increasingly more familiar with some of the spiritual concepts and ideas that evolved in Ancient Kemet (commonly known as Egypt), Kenya and Ghana in particular - all of which spoke directly to the fundamental notion of human development and socialization as a process of spiritual growth and development. It remains clear that there is a wealth of information and wisdom in the experiences and history of African people waiting to be tapped and utilized in the healing and development of African people in this country and around the world.

The symbols found on the bottom of the book cover are Adinkra Symbols developed among the Akan people in Ghana. According to W. Bruce Willis, in *The Adinkra Dictionary*, while the Adinkra Symbols evolved as a part of the mourning rituals and practices of the Akan people, they are increasingly used as a symbolic language/system for communicating the "philosophy, religious beliefs, social values and political history of the Akan people." These symbols carry with them messages about the cultural substance of a people. I offer the symbols on this book cover as a conceptual framework through which we can organize practices and systems to support the continued healing and development of African American families.

Oronde A. Miller
September 12, 2010

AN ADINKRA VALUES FRAMEWORK

(symbols featured on the book cover)

	**Gye Nyame** *"Except for God"* symbol of the supremacy of God
	**Akoben** *"War horn"* symbol of vigilance and wariness
	**Sesa Wo Suban** *"Change or transform your character"* symbol of life transformation
	**Sankofa** *"Return and get it"* symbol of importance of learning from the past
	**Akokonan** *"The leg of a hen"* symbol of nurturing and discipline
	**Aya** *"Fern"* symbol of endurance and resourcefulness
	**Mate Masie** *"What I hear, I keep"* symbol of wisdom, knowledge and prudence

Note: The explanations for the Adinkra symbols featured above are based on the descriptions provided in *The Adinkra Dictionary: A Visual Primer on the Language of Adinkra*, by W. Bruce Willis.

FACING THE RISING SUN

Introduction

"Ultimately, these essays are but one example of how each of us can find a way of reflecting on our experiences and raising our voices in the interest of improving the life experiences of children and families."

This book is a collection of essays written within the last few years. Each of the essays was inspired by my continuing reflection on both my personal involvement with this nation's foster care system, as well as my professional involvement in this nation's ongoing quest to transform child welfare practice. The essays in this book explore the meaning and significance of the African American child welfare experience primarily, and offers a framework through which this nation's system of human services can in fact become more humane in its approaches, and thus more responsive to the families and communities they are charged with supporting. Understanding some of my personal and professional background should help the reader in understanding the context in which I experience, reflect upon and make sense of this work.

My brother and I were placed in foster care at an early age in a small Ohio town. Our White mother was unable to care for us, and her relationship with our African American father was strained at best. With no support from her family, and her sincere desire for us to have a better life, she placed us in foster care with the hope that we would be adopted by a loving family that could provide for us in a way that she knew she couldn't. Our father and his family didn't find out until later. When they did find out they attempted to get us out of foster care, but were told by the authorities they were too late and were turned away.

After spending a few months in foster care in Ohio, and subsequently in Detroit, Michigan, we were adopted by a wonderful African American family in Detroit. We knew we were adopted as far back as I can remember, although I don't remember learning anything about our birth parents or those early experiences until I was an adult. I never felt growing up that my having been adopted was a strong part of my identity, or that of our family's. I also don't remember being teased about it by family members or being treated any differently as a result. We were a part of the family.

I was incredibly shy and self-conscious growing up, especially during high school and my early years in college. I was extremely nervous, guarded and quiet in relationships (especially so early on), and had a hard time trusting and confiding in others. I was very cautious about who I shared my most personal thoughts, feelings and frustrations with. I loved to debate people in classes and in organizational settings where it was always about concepts and ideas; however, I rarely exposed how I felt about things at the heart and spirit level. I am still making sense of what my personal "heart and spirit" work is about as I continue along this journey we call life. I am clear, however, that this is the part of the work that is sorely missing in the professional fields we refer to as child welfare and human services in this country.

After graduating from high school I went on to attend Howard University in Washington, D.C., where I switched academic majors from electrical engineering, to computer operated business information systems, and then to the major and minor degree programs I finally fell in love with... elementary education and African American studies, respectively. Inspired by some of my experiences studying elementary education and African American studies, I decided to forego my initial plans to teach in one of the newly formed African-centered elementary academies in Detroit and pursued my graduate studies in developmental psychology (still at Howard University).

I loved the work I was a part of, and exposed to, while working with Dr. Wade Boykin and his graduate student research team, all focused on the role of culture in shaping the schooling experiences of African American students in America's public school systems. My role in supporting that ever-evolving work continued to outpace my ability to complete my own doctoral degree requirements, and I eventually took a leave of absence, just short of completing my doctorate. I still haven't finished, but I am committed to going back and completing my degree.

It was during what was supposed to be a short break in my doctoral process that I "accidentally" started my career work in child welfare (I previously worked part-time as a counselor in an independent living program). My good friend and former professor Dr. Jaiya John was doing some consulting work at a newly formed center that was being housed under the umbrella of the Howard University School of Social Work. This new center was the National Center on Permanency for African American Children (NCPAAC). This center had recently been formed by a group of African American foster care and adoption experts, with the goal of identifying and resolving barriers to permanency for African American children in foster care.

The first big work effort of the National Center was to develop a national database of waiting African American families. Because of the Center's collective expertise, it was increasingly sought out for guidance by other organizations and agencies throughout the country. One of the larger projects the National Center committed to was a partnership with the Illinois Department of Children and Family Services to develop a local "success model" for recruiting and retaining adoptive families to care for African American children in foster care. To help develop an infrastructure to support the Center's evolving work, Jaiya assumed the role of Associate Director for the National Center, and hired me as a research associate to support the Center's research and data-related work. I had no idea at that time that I would quickly find myself involved in work that would help me to more fully understand who I am and the significance of my own personal life experiences and journey.

Given the composition of the National Center's advisory council I had an opportunity to interview and learn from the elders, as it were, of this nation's African American adoption and child welfare movement. I learned a great deal about the politics (economic, racial and cultural) of child welfare practice and policy, and more importantly about the role of racism and cultural oppression in shaping the experiences of African American children and families involved with this nation's child welfare system. It was a great and (as I appreciate more and more) truly unique environment in which to learn about child welfare.

Also during this early period, I learned that one of the pioneering adoption agencies represented on the National Center's advisory council (Homes for Black Children in Detroit, Michigan) was the actual adoption agency that brought my brother and me from Ohio and placed us in our adoptive family. I was soon informed that the National Center's staff (very small at the time) would be traveling to participate in the agency's thirty-year anniversary conference, during which I would have the opportunity to meet the founding executive director, Ms. Sydney Duncan. To this day, the moment in that hotel ballroom during which I met Sydney Duncan and her staff for the first time has been the most memorable experience I have had since being professionally involved in this work. The integrity-filled work of that adoption agency and its staff forever changed my life (and my brother's), and set me upon a life course I continue to travel. While my love and appreciation for my birth mother and father grows stronger every day, it was through the work and service of Homes for Black Children that my brother and I received the gift of family. That gift has been priceless.

Given my personal experience and the way I was introduced to child welfare practice and policy, I was very skeptical and distrustful of the professionals working in the child welfare system in general and public child welfare agencies in particular. I make a distinction between the actual public child welfare agency (which is the state and/or local government's decision-making entity that handles child protective services and foster care) and the larger child welfare system, which includes the public child welfare agency, as well as the courts, attorneys, child advocates, private community-based organizations that provide supports and services to families, mandatory reporters, therapists, and others. The work of the National Center was largely focused on identifying the historic shortcomings of the child welfare system, and highlighting the ways in which these pioneering African

American adoption agencies pushed through some of the barriers within these monstrous and bureaucratic systems.

As I gained more experience working for other local and national organizations and child welfare foundations, I continued to learn about the system's complexities, how the system has evolved over time, and the integrity and commitment of a great number of people working within these systems. There are a large number of people working to make a difference in these systems throughout the country, within very challenging environments. These individuals must be celebrated and honored for what in many cases is truly heroic work on behalf of children and their families. I also realize that commitment and good intentions among individuals working within these systems has not proven to be enough for too many of our children and families.

I've been fortunate to have had the opportunity to work directly for and alongside a number of this nation's leading national organizations, foundations and child welfare experts. Throughout these experiences my interest in and commitment to this work has always been centered around understanding and responding to the dynamics and experiences of African American children and families, and making this country's child welfare systems more effective and humane in doing the same. In doing so I've gained a greater appreciation for the similar struggles of Native American / Indian and Latino individuals and organizations who are likewise working toward equitable treatment and improved outcomes for children and families in their respective communities. Many of the ideas included in this book's essays are consistent with those advocated by individuals in these various racial and cultural communities.

My professional experiences related to understanding and resolving the inequities experienced by African American children and families involved with this nation's child welfare systems remind me a great deal of the cumulative experiences I had growing up, during my undergraduate years and also during my graduate school years at Howard University. The majority of this nation's child welfare systems (including the public agencies and their other partners and stakeholders) are still reluctant or resistant to dealing with the hard and complex dynamics of race and culture in the shaping of American society, the influence of race and culture in shaping their institutional structures and practices, as well as the relevance of race and culture in shaping the experiences of children and families involved with their systems. The same can be said of too many of the national organizations and foundations they look to for guidance and advice.

If this field is to realize its full potential and effectiveness, the people working within it will have to more fully understand and appreciate the racial and cultural underpinnings of its origins and present operations, as well as the deeper meaning and implications of race and culture in shaping the developmental experiences of the children, families and communities they purport to serve. If the field does this in a meaningful way, it is my expectation and hope that it can more fully embrace the proactive "helping" and supporting role the field is poised to play, reducing the need for the predominant and punitive "saving" (or protecting) role it tends to overwhelmingly embrace today.

My experiences working in the field thus far give me greater hope that this kind of transformation in the field of child welfare is indeed possible. It will increasingly depend, however, on child welfare professionals and social work educators opening up their training and decision-making processes to additional and previously marginalized perspectives on the work of child welfare in particular, and ideas of family and child well-being more generally. It will depend on child welfare organizations and systems opening up their doors, conference rooms, board rooms, court rooms, as well as court chambers to the children, families and communities that have been most directly impacted by their practices and policies. It will require an increased level of critically reflective practice, creative thinking and courageous risk-taking among the professionals most committed to this transformation to help move this massive system in a different direction.

The essays in this book are my way of sharing brief reflections and perspectives as I continue to engage in this work. My hope is that the various topics, perspectives and ideas shared in these essays serve as departure points, if you will, for you to dialogue more with your colleagues, classmates, friends and relatives about different aspects of African American family and child well-being in general, and the ways in which various systems in our society can more effectively support improved outcomes for children and families. Ultimately, these essays are but one example of how each of us can find a way of reflecting on our experiences and raising our voices in the interest of improving the life experiences of children and families. I thank you for your interest in this book, and hope that you find value in the ideas and perspectives contained within.

The essays that follow have not been thematically organized, although some of the essays are more closely aligned in topic and content than others. The ordering of the essays in this book follows that in which they were originally published. The final essay, *Why I Write What I Like... And Why You should Too!,* is the only essay included that was previously unpublished.

One

Renewing the Call for Activist Professionals

October 2, 2006

"There must be equally committed activists on the progressive side of policy and practice possibilities for working families in this country."

In this first essay, I'm issuing a call for a renewed sense of activism in the work of child welfare and other family and community-oriented human service professionals. I will take some time in this analysis to explore the various forms this activism might take, including the importance of consistency between our professional occupations and our personal lives. I include this reference to our personal lives because it is imperative for us to be clear and consistent in who we are so that we can show up in a genuine and authentic way as we work to support, children, youth and families.

But first, let us say a word or two about this call for increased activism. Any casual review of statistics would suggest a continuing state of crisis with respect to the day-to-day experiences of African American children, families and communities. Indeed, our families continue to struggle against tremendous odds, and are making the most of what most people agree are very difficult times... both financially and with respect to the availability of basic support services and resources from both the public and private sector.

Ironically, the general impression one gets when casually observing the news (print and visual media) and listening to the radio (particularly the music format stations) is that things: a) are as they always have been… there is no particular cause for alarm today as compared to the past; and b) people have to keep pushing on *as individuals*, so that they can get their own piece of the pie. From all appearances, people seem to be more and more focused on *trying to get their hustle on*, from the street corner to the neighborhood pulpit some might argue.

What we really want to see is a clearer sense of urgency and greater advocacy efforts on behalf of working communities, families and their children than we do by those who are antagonistic toward progressive community and family development, as well as support efforts.

There are serious activists that are unsympathetic to family preservation efforts in the child welfare community. There are serious activists that are hostile to universal health care and child care for poor and working mothers and fathers in need. There are serious activists that are hostile to practices and policies that affirm the integrity of culture and the importance of cultural continuity in child welfare placements.

There must be equally as committed activists on the progressive side of policy and practice possibilities for working families in this country!

What would this renewed and stepped-up *activist orientation* look like?

I can think of at least three vital forms of activism that have been and continue to be extremely useful to the field of child welfare and other human service professions. These are not new by any means. These are the activist values that have always undergirded segments of the child welfare profession as well as other family-oriented "helping professions."

One vital form of activism we would like to see more of is that of the **"Activist Intellectual."** The Activist Intellectual is focused on studying and communicating about the progressive needs of children and families in this country. They must also be actively involved in challenging the position of those who work against the progressive needs and interests of our poor and working families. *Activist intellectuals* will not be found exclusively in the colleges and universities. These will and must be the individuals doing and supporting the work with families in communities across this country. These critically reflective professionals are among the real experts that we should be listening to and engaging.

Another vital form of activism we must see more of is that of the **"Activist Professional."** These professionals are committed to meeting the needs of children, families and their communities, even if it means being unorthodox in their approach or going against the status quo. For these professionals families come before bureaucracies, and before institutional barriers and stumbling blocks. Activist professionals make it their responsibility to shine a light on - and resolve - institutional challenges when doing such is necessary to meet the needs of families. They go the extra mile to find the resources families really need, even when not readily available. They create the programs and structures that are necessary to do progressive work.

It is also possible that these professionals might not be *in the trenches,* if you will. They might work for national non-profits, foundations or other organizations, but are committed in their roles to supporting the progressive interests, and meeting the real needs, of children and families. These individuals are often the "gatekeepers" of financial and other resources that are desperately needed by individuals that are, in fact, *in the trenches* doing the work.

A final vital form of activism can be described as that of the **"Activist Leader and/or Policy Maker."** These are the individuals that are responsible for passing laws and securing the essential resources needed to support our priorities. They make policies that affirm and protect the real needs and interests of children, families and communities. They speak truth to power. They stand tall and represent the progressive interests of our families and communities. They pro-actively trouble-shoot and problem-solve so that others can be more effective in their work. They observe, listen and reflect. Only then do they begin to offer their ideas.

One thing all of these activist individuals have in common is their commitment and passion for making a positive difference on behalf of African American families and children. They are all committed to doing everything possible (not only things convenient and "permitted") to meet the needs of families and communities. They make a way when there is no way. They think outside of the box. They challenge the status quo. By definition, they tend not to be *conservative* when problem-solving. They support what works best in meeting the real needs of children, families and communities today.

The ideas I have mentioned in this essay are not new ideas. These ideas and the kinds of people described above have always existed in this work, and do today as well. They are the examples… *the Exemplars…* that we must make ourselves familiar with. We stand to learn a lot from their work, experiences and reflections.

We need to see evidence of more of these types of individuals and a renewed sense of urgency when it comes to our families. This cannot only be the work we do in our "professional" lives… or in our "spare" time. I would argue that it must be our focus in both our professional and personal lives.

We must see more progressive and explicit support for the issues and causes that highlight and respond to the lived realities of our families that continue to struggle. Moreover, we are calling for increased support (financial and otherwise) for organizations that fight hard every day to improve the lives of our children and families.

The need is great. We must be clear about the great sense of urgency. I hope these words have meant something to you, and that they have encouraged you to reflect critically about these issues and dynamics. As many of you know firsthand our children and our families continue to struggle. All of us *can* do more! All of us *must* do more! *Aluta Continua (The Struggle Continues)!*

Two

Permanency Matters! Affirming Every Child's Existence in this World

October 9, 2006

"...everyone, at the most fundamental level, needs t know that their existence in this universe is acknowledged, affirmed and celebrated by someone else somewhere in this world."

In this essay I will explain, at a fundamental level, why permanency is so important for children. To do so I would like to share a recent experience with you that, for me, highlights a very basic, yet so important dynamic of permanency. For these purposes I'll be considering my own adoption experience, yet what I'm trying to articulate is not really about me nor is it unique to adoption.

We should also be mindful that permanency can include so many other types of relationships, including reunification with birth parents, kinship care, guardianship, as well as other forms of "permanent" relationships. But we'll talk about that a bit more at some other time.

My older brother, Khari, and I grew up in Detroit, Michigan after being adopted when we were 1 and 2 years old, respectively. After graduating from high school, I went off to Washington, DC for college and have lived and worked in the metropolitan Washington DC area ever since.

I traveled home to Detroit, Michigan a few weeks ago to attend a meeting, and had a chance to visit my parents and brother for a couple of days before and after the meeting. My parents had just recently bought a new house and were beginning the process of packing and preparing to move.

When I arrived, the first thing I noticed was that all of the art work had been taken off the walls and packed for moving. As I walked upstairs, I noticed that all of the pictures had also been taken down for the move. This really stood out because my parents had a lot of family photos tucked inside of frames and displayed all throughout the house.

As we grew up so many of the family photos were of my immediate family as well as other relatives and family friends. Several years ago, I had the privilege of marrying my wife, Amina, and we now have two children, five and three years old. As you could expect many of the photos in my parents' house are now of the expanding family (especially the grandchildren), with a sprinkling of some of the older family photos still around as well. I know very well how excited our children get when they go see their grandparents and they get to see all of the photos of them throughout the house, from birth through the present.

When I visited a few weeks ago it really struck me how bare the walls were, and that the images were no longer up on the walls. It was at that moment that something very basic struck me about this thing we call permanency.

One of the basic reasons permanency is so important is that everyone, at the most fundamental level, needs to know that their existence in this universe is acknowledged, affirmed and celebrated by someone else somewhere in this world. Realizing the pictures were not on the wall reminded me how much I value the fact that my parents have always been there for me, have always loved me, and have always celebrated me and embraced me for who I am, even as I continued to grow and evolve over time. This basic truth is on display all the time in their house, capturing our growth through each developmental stage of our lives, and now those of my children and wife.

That moment reminded me how fortunate my brother and I have been. It also reminded me how fortunate our daughter and son are in comparison to so many thousands of African American children that continue to languish in this nation's foster care system.

While I have always realized and appreciated how fortunate my brother and I have been, I was not always as clear about the *meaning* of our experience, specifically the meaning inherent in our adoption experience.

Unlike too many adoptees, Khari and I always knew we were adopted. Our parents told us when we were very young and it never figured very prominently in my childhood and adolescent years. Certainly, I was thankful for all that our parents had done and provided for us along the way. It wasn't until I was in graduate school and began working in the field of child welfare, however, that I really began to appreciate the deeper meaning and significance of having been adopted.

Looking at family photos on the wall would be fairly unremarkable for many people. But hundreds of thousands of children in this country, disproportionately African American, have been shuffled from one stranger's (foster) home to another, a pattern that has continued sometimes for more than 15-17 years of their lives—their entire childhood. Many of us can only imagine what that must feel like.

Many of us look at something as normal as family photos on our walls and start to reminisce about the good times from different phases of our lives. We think about our childhood years playing with and learning from our mother and father, our siblings, cousins, friends, etc. But so many children can only imagine what that is like. They imagine that their mothers and fathers still exist somewhere out there in the world, but they really don't know for sure. They wonder if they have siblings out there somewhere, but unlike many of us, they can only wonder. All too often, they think about their friends with bittersweet emotion. Many of their closest childhood friendships get cut way too short with each change in foster care placement. Indeed, the notion of friendships takes on a different kind of meaning with these experiences.

I realize that not every foster care experience is the same. But so many foster care experiences are characterized by extreme instability and insecurity. For many children in foster care *permanency* is but an abstract concept, a term used by social workers and legal representatives.

But what I know for certain is that all children need to be able to grow up and go out into the world, knowing that they belong somewhere and belong to someone. We all need to know that somewhere in the world there are other individuals that know who we are, care about us, and will be there for us in our times of struggle and need. We all need to know that our existence matters to someone else, and that we can always go back to that place we call home when times get rough, or when we just need to recharge and get centered again.

This is what I was reminded of when I was home. I know where home is because I see a representation of my reality expressed in so many different ways throughout the house. I see the funny outfits, the funny expressions, the proud moments of celebration, and so much more. More than anything else, I know that someone there cares about me and takes pride in celebrating my existence.

This is why permanency matters. This is why we must rededicate ourselves to making permanency a reality for the many thousands of children that wonder and wait. Our children are crying out for us. We must reclaim our children and bring them home.

Three

Reflecting on the King Holiday: Will *We* Be Caught Sleeping Through a Great Revolution?

January 17, 2007

"The theme that ran through this sermon... was the critical and active role each and every one of us must play in making this a country that is compassionate, equitable and morally just."

I'd like to take this time to reflect on the recent holiday celebrating the life and legacy of the Rev. Dr. Martin Luther King, Jr. The Monday holiday is a day that I have used for many years now as an opportunity for reflection, contemplation, and more recently, a periodic reassessment of how I use my time, skills and talents to help make this world a better place for children and families today, and the generations of children that have yet to be born.

I began this ritual when I was in high school, and have continued annually in one form or another. I am even more proud to do this now with my children as they continue to grow and become ever more inquisitive about what daddy is doing and what daddy is listening to.

As is my routine, I began this year's holiday listening to some of the morning radio and television shows to get a sense of what the "popular coverage" of the King Holiday would offer. As is increasingly the case, I was greatly disappointed at the public discourse on the meaning and contemporary implications of Dr. King's life, words, work and legacy. The public and popular discourse gets more disappointing every year. This is unfortunate because so much of what people, particularly children, in this country come to know about history and contemporary society is learned via some sort of popular media.

After listening to some of the morning coverage of this year's holiday, I used the remainder of the day, off and on, listening to some of the major speeches that Dr. King delivered during his lifetime. In recent years I have found myself listening to speeches and sermons delivered during the last year of Dr. King's very short life, especially those delivered during 1968 in the last few months of his life.

One of the speeches that I listened to today was a sermon Dr. King delivered on March 31, 1968 at the Washington

National Cathedral in Washington, DC. This sermon is popularly referred to as "Remaining Awake Through a Great Revolution." In this sermon Dr. King addressed a broad range of issues, including persistent hunger and poverty, the idea of affirmative action and the "bootstrap" analysis of African American progress, as well as a critical analysis of this nation's greatest contradiction of that day… the Vietnam War as contrasted with the domestic challenges of the United States during and leading up to the year 1968.

The theme that ran through this sermon, as with many of Dr. King's sermons, was the critical and active role each and every one of us must play in making this a country that is compassionate, equitable and morally just. Dr. King was clear that this was and continues to be both a moral as well as a practical necessity if we desire a world and nation that is safe and healthy for our children, families and communities. Given the increasingly hostile climate in this nation's domestic and foreign affairs the consequences of inaction *or even ineffective action* could be a society that continues to slide towards chaos and "potential annihilation" (as Dr. King quite appropriately put it). While this sermon spoke of American society at-large and the relationship of the African American community to it, the analysis is just as relevant to the state of affairs *within* the African American community.

While listening and reflecting I found myself drawing parallels between the words Dr. King spoke during this sermon and the present-day challenges we face in this society in general, and more specifically, the dynamics we continue to struggle with in the work of child welfare and human services.

Much of the discussion about the challenges of the current child welfare field centers around the specific practices professionals are engaged in on a daily basis. I don't think this is completely off base, but I think the underlying issues in child welfare are much deeper than the specific practices professionals engage in. I believe the underlying challenges facing child welfare and human services more broadly in this country are rooted in the fundamental values of this society, and the underlying assumptions about the value and utility of support for certain children, families and communities relative to others. These values and assumptions are largely shaped by this country's legacy of *structural, institutional and individual racism.*

As Dr. King so eloquently pointed out, African American families and communities are, and always have been, undervalued and scorned in this society. There continues to be very little value associated with the life experiences of African American families and children by this nation and its institutions, including private and government institutions. Thus, little value is often seen in providing supports and resources to help change the real conditions and circumstances that so many of our families and communities are forced to endure. It remains our challenge to turn this reality on its ugly head, and provide the supports necessary to develop, strengthen and celebrate our children, families and communities.

I would also like to highlight yet another one of the critical messages shared by Dr. King in the sermon mentioned above and so many other sermons he delivered, increasingly so in the latter period of his life. We must recall Dr. King's critical assessment of the involvement of White people in the struggle for racial equity and justice in this country. White people in this society must ask themselves if they are truly committed to the cause of racial equity and justice, and how they "show up" in this enduring struggle.

It is my opinion that there is a role for truly committed anti-racist "allies" that are indeed willing to "wave the flag" and speak truth to power. These flags, however, shouldn't be waved opportunistically by Whites only while standing side by side with African Americans for photo-ops or in African American pulpits on Sunday mornings during election season. This commitment, dedication and courage is needed in the boardrooms, courtrooms, media outlets as well as political and financial institutions… especially when we are not there to hear and offer congratulatory praise.

We need to see more examples… exemplars... of the courage demonstrated by Dr. Martin Luther King, Jr. Every one of us has an opportunity to speak our truth to power, but it won't happen by simply dreaming about it. Let us all affirm the real legacy of Dr. Martin Luther King, Jr. by recommitting ourselves to the noble work of healing families and communities. Let us celebrate his example of activism and protest... and not just the rhetorical dream. The promise of a better tomorrow begins with us.

Four

Affirming Every Child's Existence: Child Welfare Beyond Child Protection and Intervention

April 19, 2007

"What institutional mechanisms do we have in place to support and enhance the developmental experiences of this large number of families and their children, especially poor and/or African American?"

Several months ago (October 9, 2006) I wrote an essay about the importance of permanency for children in foster care. One of the points I tried to make in that essay was that all children deserve to have their existence recognized in a positive, loving and affirming way by someone else somewhere in this world.

In that essay I reflected upon my experience growing up as an adopted child. I reflected on the significance of the small things that many of us take for granted, such as going back home as an adult and seeing my childhood pictures hanging up on the wall and in photo albums in my parents' house. As an adult, I continue to know that my reality matters to someone else in this world… that someone else in this world acknowledges and celebrates my very existence.

In that essay much of the tone and perspective was written in the context of permanency; more specifically my experience growing up adopted. In this essay I would like to reflect on this same dynamic, but broaden it to all children and families… not only children who were adopted, or families and children involved in this nation's child protection and foster care systems.

As I have stated previously, everyone, at the most fundamental level, needs to know that their existence is acknowledged, affirmed and celebrated by someone else in this world.

There are many things that many of us take for granted as adults. Having meaningful relationships with other individuals is one of those things. We know that many children with foster care experience throughout this country, through no fault of their own, go through the rest of their lives without being able to effectively develop and sustain such relationships. This is but one relationship dynamic that frequently results from growing up in less stable, less supportive and less nurturing environments.

This experience, however, is shared by many children and adults that have no foster care experience at all. Not all families that "stay together" necessarily provide the most nurturing and supportive environments.

When I refer to family and child well-being I am talking about more than just the well-being of families and children caught up in this nation's child protection and foster care systems. I am talking about the well-being of all children, families and communities. We cannot assume that all children who grow up without child welfare system intervention in fact enjoy the benefits of a healthy, nurturing and affirming family environment. Most of us need not look very far to see this.

One of our collective challenges is to ensure that all children grow up in a supportive, nurturing and healthy environment. What institutional mechanisms do we have in place to support and enhance the developmental experiences of this large number of families and their children, especially poor and African American? All of us can play a role in making this a reality, including public child welfare systems throughout the country.

Indeed, no single person, organization or institution can do everything; however, every one of us can do something. And I suspect that many of us can do more than we are currently.

As I mentioned, public child welfare systems also have a role to play. Granted, this would mean a broadening of the mission and purpose of many of this nation's public child welfare agencies/systems, but it is very much possible and necessary.

Public child welfare agencies throughout this country were created in the spirit of "saving children" from what "professionals" deemed (and still deem) to be unsafe home environments and unfit parents. The challenge of child welfare in this country has often been discussed within the context of how to most efficiently and effectively "protect" children from abusive and neglectful parents. Child welfare systems have not generally allocated substantial resources to support the development and strengthening of families not seen as needing emergency intervention. Nor has this even been a significant component of most public agencies' broader mission and purpose.

Many public child welfare systems searching for ways to reduce racial disproportionality and racially disparate outcomes in their respective child welfare systems (to their credit) are beginning to explore these very dynamics within their respective child welfare systems. They are finding that diverting many families to appropriate community-based services and programs, before CPS intervention is deemed necessary, significantly improves the outcomes and well-being of the families and communities involved.

Indeed this speaks to a different role for most public child welfare systems. It requires public child welfare agencies to become more familiar with the strengths, assets and resources available within communities. It requires the public child welfare agency to develop partnerships with many of the community organizations, community leaders and community organizers they have up until now been less familiar with.

Moreover, it speaks to the need for greater flexibility by child welfare agencies (and human service systems more broadly) in deciding how to allocate resources to most effectively respond to the real needs of children and families… *before a crisis emerges.*

Public child welfare systems moving in this direction should be commended for their efforts, as well as encouraged to continue expanding these efforts. Other child welfare systems should be encouraged to move in this direction. Child welfare systems cannot do it alone. Nor are they likely to sustain such efforts without the continuous oversight, pressure and commitment from the broader community and community-based organizations.

The challenge confronting us is clear. The sense of urgency is also clear to those of us close to this work. Let our collective action tell the story of our community's determination and commitment to our families. Let our determination and collective action affirm the right of our children to exist and develop to their fullest potential.

Five

Kinship Care *Down In The Delta*... Celebrating A Tradition of Family Taking Care of Family

April 30, 2007

"Let us be reminded that none of our families is perfect. We should also not expect perfection from our many families struggling against real challenges."

Across the country there are families struggling to keep it together. Many of these families come to the attention of the child welfare system for various reasons. The majority of the Caucasian families that come to the attention of child protective services are referred because of suspicion of physical and sexual abuse. For African American families it is more frequently the suspicion of some form of neglect.

When the allegations are substantiated, Caucasian families are more frequently offered family preservation services in an effort to keep their families intact. African American families are more often separated, with the children coming into the formal foster care system. This decision by presumably well-intentioned social workers marks the beginning of what too often becomes a career in foster care, in many cases spanning an entire childhood. Indeed, this is unacceptable and doesn't have to be the case. There are other viable and more constructive alternatives. Consider the following all-too-familiar scenario…

A relatively young (mid-thirties) and unmarried woman lives with her mother, pre-adolescent son and pre-toddler daughter in Chicago. She is unemployed, largely undereducated and seemingly locked in a cycle of poverty, despair and depression. While she really does want to work and provide for her children, she really is not confident in her ability to do so, nor does she really know where to start. Most of her efforts to acquire even basic employment are either unsuccessful or met with rejection, personal humiliation and embarrassment. She often numbs the hurt and passes her days away high on either drugs, alcohol or both. As you can imagine, she has no difficulty at all finding the corner liquor store and/or neighborhood drug dealer.

This woman's mother and son are both extremely supportive of her. Yet, they are simultaneously frustrated and appear to be running out of patience. They know that she is really not being herself, and is just a shell of the person she once was. But they continue to be there for her, knowing that it's just a matter of time before she gets her act together again. Rock bottom is sure to come, but they just don't know when. Through it all, they always keep that door of hope and possibility open, waiting and waiting for what might sometimes seem to be a distant miracle.

As a last resort and desperate measure, the grandmother sends the family down south to live with relatives. This gets the children out of the dangerous and unhealthy circumstances they currently live in, and gives the mother some time and space to "get her act together."

This is one aspect of the storyline to the 1998 motion picture *Down in the Delta*, starring Alfre Woodard and Al Freeman, Jr., among others. Different versions of this basic story line play out every day in many families in communities across America, including the African American community. Certainly, resilience is a central theme of our history and experience living in this country. Unlike the scenario depicted in this movie, however, many such families today come to the attention of this nation's overwhelmingly punitive public child welfare system.

In 1977, Dr. Robert Hill published the results of a research effort documenting the practice, among African American families, of caring for their relatives during hard times. This tradition of informal adoption and the centrality of extended family support systems in the African American community has been around for centuries, dating back to our pre-America family patterns in Africa and other parts of the

African diaspora. In more recent years, the child welfare field "discovered" this pattern and named it *Kinship Care.*

There are a few brief points I would like to make in this essay. They are not new points, but ones that I think we should continue to uplift in our work, and in our conversations about family and child well-being.

First, I encourage all of you to buy and/or rent a copy of *Down in the Delta.* We have to search hard, high and low for quality images and stories highlighting the integrity, perseverance and hope that characterize the African American experience. This story is a classic story depicting the African American spirit of resilience, spirituality, the value of hard work and education as well as the resourcefulness of the extended family. These are among the characteristics discussed in Dr. Robert Hill's 1972 book, *Strengths of African American Families* (republished in 1997).

More than to express my appreciation for this movie, I have also written this essay as a reminder that while families might be struggling and while children may at times even be at risk of harm, parents are often trying their best to make some sense out of extremely challenging life situations. While all of this is going on, there are often other relatives willing, even if hesitant, to step in and support the child and parents.

Too often, the furthest we tend to look is for grandparents. As great a resource as grandparents often are, they are not the only relatives who can support the process. We must broaden our search efforts to identify cousins, aunts, uncles, brothers, sisters and other individuals who may not be blood relatives, but are just as close to and supportive of the family. Our search must also reach beyond the artificial borders of city, county and state. Family ties are spread out around this country, and so must our search efforts follow these ties. Policies regarding inter-jurisdictional placements and kinship care funding must be responsive to this dynamic.

How ironic that we keep children in foster care for years and defend a worker's assertion that she or he cannot find any relatives, yet when many of the children age out of foster care they go right back to their parent or some other member of their extended family support network. Moreover, many children who "run away" while in care similarly "run to" the same family members.

There is a familiar saying that people evoke when arguing against the practice of "kinship care." It states that "*the fruit don't fall far from the tree*." Well, I am also clear that you can make some real good pie, preserves and more from all of a tree's fruit, be it picked off the tree or picked off the ground. Moreover, as my Aunt Ruth and Uncle David taught me as a little child playing by the pear tree in their back yard, during some years the tree's yield may leave us wanting and wondering; but, we will keep going back to the same tree every year expecting the best. And so it is with life and family.

Let us be reminded that none of our families are perfect. Likewise, we should also not require perfection from the families struggling against real life challenges, and who may be involved with this nation's child welfare system. Let's start providing families with the real supports they need!

Six

A Celebration of African American Mothers!

May 22, 2007

"You are a part of a very strong and proud tradition of African American mothers that have always been on the front lines of our community's struggles in this country."

In this issue I would like to celebrate the significance of African American mothers and their immeasurable contribution to the history and continued development of African American families. I would like to do so in a very personal way, by reflecting on my relationship with my mother. I debated whether to share this personal message in this way, but ultimately decided to do so.

This tribute is written as a letter to my mother, expressing my great appreciation and admiration for who she is and what she has meant to me over the years. I am also hoping, however, to celebrate the critical contribution and role of African American mothers who keep hanging in there. Fathers are equally important, but this is my moment to say "thank you" to the mothers.

Dear Mom, there are many things I can say to describe how much (and why) I respect you, appreciate you and love you. You have been so many different things for Khari and me over the years.

When we were younger, you were our healer during those late nights and weekends when we were sick. You were the judge and the jury when we got into trouble. You disciplined us in the moment when we misbehaved, making sure we knew exactly why we were in trouble *and* what conduct would have been more appropriate. When we were really bad, you made sure Dad heard about it and had his say.

You were a teacher and tutor to us, making sure we excelled in all of our classes. You made sure that we knew college was easily within our potential and certain to be within our reach. You knew our potential and expected/accepted nothing short of excellence.

On this occasion, Mom, I really just want to say thank you! Not because you struggled as a single mother through endless years of poverty doing it all alone. Not because you put all of your hopes and dreams into an entertainment career in search of that big break. And not because you fought your way through the mean streets, “pulling yourself up by your bootstraps," to become that great national symbol of perseverance and self-reliance. Perhaps there is a place for all of these stories, but these tend to be the only "feel good" stories we see on the rags-to-riches television specials celebrating triumph over adversity. There are many other everyday stories of integrity and honor to be told and examples to be shared. Yours is one of those stories.

Mom, I thank you on this occasion because you are like so many other African American mothers out there that do your thing with no real national and community celebration... having grown up among a generation of African American families in a home that emphasized the values of hard work, continuous education and a steadfast faith and belief in God. You are like so many African American mothers that have always found a way to make things work, despite the many challenges that life tends to present.

I thank you because you have lived a life of service… committing your professional life to educating children, and supporting other professionals in their efforts to do the same. I thank you because you have always been committed to living a life *on* purpose and *of* integrity. I thank you because you have always been consistent. I thank you for your example of how to care for and "be there" for family members and friends in times of need.

I thank you for showing us how to rely on others for support and assistance, both during life's day-to-day routines and the challenging circumstances that we all face from time to time. I also appreciate your insistence that we be there and willing to sacrifice and open up our home for other friends and relatives when needed. By example you have demonstrated that we must be humble, caring, giving and compassionate in our conduct and in our relationships with others.

You have done all of this and so much more. You have given up so much of yourself over the years without even the slightest hint of regret. You have made it clear on many occasions that you have done it all out of love and your commitment to ensuring that we had access to the best this world has to offer.

Mom, I also thank you for doing what too many mothers have for some reason been reluctant to do… you instilled within Khari and me a great appreciation of what it means to be of African ancestry in America. I thank you for exposing us to and raising us in a household that celebrates African and African American beauty, art and music; that celebrates the accomplishments of great African and African American leaders and achievers; that consciously celebrates and actively contributes to our rich legacy of civic, social and political engagement and activism.

While your life story may not be the rags-to-riches story people celebrate on television, I am also very clear that yours has not been an easy journey by any means. You have worked very hard, and have endured your share of life's challenging circumstances.

In his poem *Mother to Son,* Langston Hughes was correct when describing that *"life for (you) ain't been no crystal stair. (I know that) it's had tacks in it, and splinters, and boards torn up! But all the time (you) been a-climbin' on, and reachin' landin's, and turnin' corners, and sometimes goin' in the dark where there ain't been no light."* The one thing I can tell you for sure, mom, is that you never have to worry about me turning back or setting down on steps, whenever life gets kind of hard. Indeed I will always keep going, and just as you showed us, you will always find me, *"still climbin'."*

I must acknowledge that one very basic reason I am committed to the preservation of the Black family today is that I know its value (despite the way this great tradition is disrespected and violated daily). I know very well that thirty five years ago on this very day, the lives of two little Black babies hung in the balance. The scales could have easily tipped one way or the other. For a brief moment, in fact, the scales were leaning a different way. My life could easily have been completely different, but for a Black family's choice. You and Dad, and both of your extended families, chose us, so that we might have a better life. And I will forever be thankful for it. I wake up every morning and give thanks for all that you and Dad have made possible for us. Given our experience, I certainly appreciate the significance of adoption. Adoption can be great for some children and families; however, not every adoptee can claim the blessings Khari and I have been showered with. What I wish to emphasize here is my true appreciation for the substance of *who* you are, and *how* you are.

I know, because of your example, our purpose in life is not to make endless amounts of money in order to consume and acquire more objects. We are here to provide for and care for our children, families and communities. We are here to prepare our children for a life *of and on* purpose, and to contribute to making our communities stronger. You have demonstrated that we can do all of this while still living an enjoyable and rewarding life.

You are a part of a very strong and proud tradition of African American mothers that have always been on the front lines of our community's struggles in this country. You have made your contribution with grace and dignity. On this day I thank you, Mom, for your example and all that you are. *I Love You!*

Seven

A Celebration of African American Fathers

June 22, 2007

"...even our personal goals must be in support of our families, the larger community and unequivocally in support of the continued healing and development of the African American community."

In this issue I would like to celebrate the significance of African American fathers and their immeasurable contribution to the history and continued development of African American families. I will do so in a very personal way by reflecting, in the form of a letter, on my relationship with my father.

As was the case with my celebration of mothers, this essay is also a difficult one to write, as these reflections are very personal. After experiencing the last six years of fatherhood, I am clear that African American fathers are likely among the most misrepresented and misunderstood groups of people. *But still we rise!*

Dear Dad, there are few public representations of African American fathers that shed light on the strength and integrity of our experience. Most of the depictions that claim to capture the personal side of fathers only talk about our pains, missteps and tribulations, and how we struggle just to stay alive and find meaning in life. Well there is another story that needs to be told. I would like to reflect on the tremendous passion and courage that exemplifies African American fatherhood, and the sacrifice that so many African American fathers make every day to ensure that our children, families and communities are well. This is a reflection on men like you.

This essay can't undo all of the craziness people say about African American fathers, but it is a way for me to say thank you and celebrate all that you have meant to me. As with my recent reflections about mom, there are likewise many reasons for me to thank you for being a great father.

I am deeply appreciative of the discipline you helped to instill in Khari and me. You always insisted that we listen to and show respect for mom, other adults (especially women) and our elders. These values and rules were non-negotiable. You made it clear that our behavior didn't only reflect on us as individuals, but also our family and our community, including the rich, proud legacy of our ancestors.

I have to tell you that of all our friends you were always seen as one of the strictest fathers. Physically you have always had a commanding presence and you had minimal tolerance for nonsense and foolishness with us and our friends as we were growing up. I realize now that one big reason for that was that the stakes were (and continue to be) too high for African American youth getting caught up in otherwise typical adolescent nonsense.

While you were strict and quick to discipline us for getting into trouble, you have always been a very fun and affectionate father as well. I remember those many nights you came home after we were in bed, came into the bedroom, closed the door quietly behind you, and scared the mess out of us by making strange noises. Then you'd start tickling us and wrestling with us until we were either too tired or started crying from laughter. You would then tuck us back in and kiss us goodnight. Those were great days and nights.

You also made sure we did recreational and other fun activities together as a family, including tennis, swimming, badminton, family pizza and game nights, as well as other family outings and vacations.

On the serious side, I remain thankful for the effort you made to expose me as an adolescent to some of the service activities of the Detroit Alumni Chapter of Kappa Alpha Psi Fraternity, Inc. It was my involvement with the Detroit Kappa League that showed me the real potential of African American social and civic organizations, *when they are committed to ideals higher themselves.* The African American men I was exposed to through this experience demonstrated the values of sacrifice, discipline, hard work, education, service and achievement. More importantly, however, these men were not committed to a selfish kind of individual and personal achievement, but made it clear that even our personal goals must be in support of our families, the larger community and unequivocally in support of the continued healing and development of the African American community.

I am equally thankful for the examples of fatherhood found in my other cousins, uncles and extended family growing up. You all have been devoted fathers, protecting us as best you could from the madness in the streets, and ensuring that we followed a path to success and self-sufficiency for ourselves and now our families.

Dad, I frequently find myself thinking about the crisis-oriented state of affairs facing African American youth, families and communities. I find myself reflecting on the climate growing up in 1970's and 1980's Detroit. This was the period that teenage gun violence started to skyrocket to unprecedented and senseless levels.

It is with this in mind that I appreciate all of the lectures and other steps you and mom took to keep Khari and me from getting too caught up in that pathology. I appreciate and respect the way you intervened to de-escalate that petty neighborhood beef when we were in high school. You got us and the other family to sit down and talk through the senseless drama that could very easily have resulted in more Black teenage gun violence. I can appreciate that in all of your years as a middle and high school guidance counselor and principal in the Detroit Public Schools, you have seen your share of what that pathology has produced, and the pain and heartbreak it has inflicted on families.

I remember when you sat me down in the family room and shared with me some of your observations of the American political and criminal justice systems, especially as they relate to African American families. Your message was neither one exclusively about "personal responsibility" nor one exclusively about "blaming the system." Instead your message was about critical observation, critical study, and critical reflection, as well as our responsibility to be socially and politically aware and engaged. Through your words and your example, you demonstrated what it means to be actively engaged, to see and understand things within their historical context, and to work with integrity in the interests of African American families and communities.

There's another big lesson you taught me. I can't remember what I was struggling with, but you shared with me that the most difficult aspect of any decision is actually making it. You went on to share the importance of weighing your options, and then moving forward with the option that feels most comfortable. You told me to put fear aside and don't get stuck thinking about all of the "what ifs." You said that even when the decision is wrong, you can at least try to correct it and move on. But you have to actually get through the decision-making process to have that opportunity.

I have come to appreciate that even when we exercise poor judgment and/or make unwise decisions, the great thing is that we frequently have time and are given opportunities to work through the consequences. It might take some time, but that's the beauty of life... our experiences produce opportunities for learning and growth. Perfection is not required in order to be a good person, always seeking to be better and to do better. I appreciate your lessons and your example.

Dad, you and mom have blessed Khari and me in immeasurable ways. Your example of how to live life through the easy times and the difficult times has been priceless. If I can build on the example the two of you have provided, I am confident that I will also be a great father like you! *Thank you again, and I Love You!*

Eight

Redefining the Mission of Child Welfare Systems: Working for Family and Child Well-Being!

August 22, 2007

"Ultimately, this country needs more than an improved child welfare system. We need a fundamentally revamped set of economic and human service systems that truly promote the well-being of family and community."

A report released earlier this year by UNICEF ranked twenty-one economically advanced countries according to six measures of child well-being. The report, *Child Poverty in Perspective: An Overview of Child Well-Being in Rich Countries*, ranked countries according to levels of material well-being, health and safety, educational well-being, family and peer relationships, behaviors and risks, and subjective well-being.

Not surprisingly (to many of us at least) the United States was ranked among the lowest of the ranked countries. Only Great Britain was worse in the average rankings. In fact, according to the report, "Great Britain and the United States find themselves in the bottom third of the rankings for five of the six dimensions reviewed."

Even a casual review of national trends regarding child well-being confirms the above-mentioned report's conclusions, and should be cause for alarm. Just last month the Annie E. Casey Foundation released the 2007 Kids Count report detailing the current state of child well-being in this country. The results, covering 10 indicators of child well-being, continue to be alarming. Moreover, according to the report, "the size of the gap between black and non-Hispanic White children varies by indicator, but the outcomes for black children are worse on every one of the 10 indicators."

Among the indicators… One in three (36%) African American children in this country live in poverty (income below $19,806 for a family of two adults and 2 children), more than three times the percentage for White children and almost double the percentage for all children. The African American infant mortality rate is 13.8 per 1,000 live births, more than twice the national average and almost 2.5 times the rate for White infants.

This data notwithstanding, there are still many African American families and children doing very well, and as I have mentioned previously, thriving against tremendous odds.

Through this essay I want to strongly encourage all of us to reflect more seriously on the kind of society we live in, and the kinds of systems that would be necessary to truly respond to the challenges of struggling families in this country. More specifically, there is an extremely urgent need for us to develop culturally responsive strategies to significantly improve African American child and family well-being.

For those of us working in the child welfare system, it is our obligation to use all of our power and influence to ensure that African American families in need receive the supports that would truly be effective, not just those that have typically been made available. These services and supports are particularly necessary at the earliest stages of a family's contact with the child protection and foster care systems.

Relevant services would include (but not be limited to) safe and affordable high quality housing; proven effective substance abuse treatment and rehabilitation programs, effective mental health services comparable to those accessible by families "with means;" stable and family-friendly employment opportunities that pay a living wage; access to free and/or affordable child care; relevant job training and educational advancement programs; safe and publicly accessible recreation and athletic facilities; as well as free comprehensive health care coverage for all families. Far from exhaustive, the above list would at least make for a good start.

Before a child is removed from her or his family it is imperative that we exhaust all of the support services practical, available and necessary. There is nothing more sacred in the realm of African American childhood relationships than the relationship of an African American child to her or his family and community.

When a child must be removed from her or his parents' home, it is our obligation to find relative caregivers or members of the extended family support network that would be appropriate resource families while the parents work on their challenges. We must ensure that these kinship caregivers and guardianship resource families get *at least* the same financial resources afforded non-relative (stranger) foster families.

When out of home care is necessary, truly effective support and coordination programs must simultaneously be in place so that birth parents working on their challenges can have constructive interactions with their children and other family members. Experience has demonstrated, and research has documented, that this results in (expedited) family reunification when coordinated effectively.

Our challenge is not just to make the child welfare system that we have known in this society for decades work better. We must leave open for consideration that the foundational values upon which the modern day child welfare system rests is in fact contradictory to the aims of the system reform and transformation efforts many of us work toward… in fact contradictory to the aim of promoting family and child well-being.

I argue that we must articulate the foundational values that should undergird a truly effective and responsive *set of systems* that promote comprehensive community development and family well-being. At that point we can identify the real services and support resources families and communities frequently need, and develop the structures and institutions that can provide those supports and services effectively and equitable to the need.

Ultimately, this country needs more than an improved child welfare system. We need a fundamentally revamped set of economic and human service systems that truly promote the well-being of family and community. My interactions with families, as well as child welfare and other human service professionals around this country, suggests that this is indeed a possibility.

I firmly believe this country is at a crossroads. We have the know-how and the resources to make this vision a reality. The critical question is whether we have the will, the courage and commitment to do it. Our challenge is to make our voices heard so that individuals with similar ideas can align resources and work together. This is our generation's challenge. We *can* do this! We *must* do this! And we must do so *in our lifetime*!

Nine

Jena 6: An Overview and Critical Analysis

September 20, 2007

"Tension between Whites and Blacks is not new to Jena, Louisiana. According to reports, there are still very clear and historic patterns of explicit racism and segregation still in place in 2007."

The Institute for Family and Child Well-Being has as a part of its focus the experiences of children and families caught in the web of both the child welfare and juvenile justice systems in this country. Given my personal and professional experiences, the child welfare system has been the subject of the majority of my *Perspectives* essays to-date.

In this essay, and on this day of protest and resistance, I would like to take a critical look at the tragic injustice that has been unfolding in Jena, Louisiana. I will start by providing a general overview of, and critical commentary about, the major events and timelines connected with the Jena, Louisiana controversy. I will also attempt to place these tragic *Jena 6* experiences in a national context, as they exemplify many aspects of this nation's juvenile and criminal justice systems that have been and continue to be racist, oppressive, unjust and hurtful to African American families and communities. I conclude with reflections on what these incidents and the unfolding national response might mean for the ongoing African American struggle against racism and cultural oppression in this country.

Jena 6: An Overview and Timeline

Jena 6 refers to the six African American students (and their families) that are currently caught up in the criminal justice system in Jena, Louisiana for their part in a series of racially-charged incidents in Jena, Louisiana. The following is a general description and timeline I've been able to piece together of the major events connected with the *Jena 6*.

Pre-September 2006: Tension between Whites and Blacks is not new to Jena, Louisiana. According to reports, there are still very clear and historic patterns of explicit racism and segregation still in place in 2007. Some White residents in Jena boast openly about their historic and present-day "Whites only" preferences, practices, and policies. While there has always been resistance to these trends, these social patterns remain the norm for many in Jena, Louisiana.

Late August / September 2006: A Black student asked the Jena High School principal for permission to sit under a tree in the school's courtyard that had been historically designated as a "Whites only" tree. The principal advised the students that anyone can sit under the tree. Several Black students did. The next day, three nooses were found hanging from the tree. For anyone less familiar, the noose has for generations been used as a symbol of hatred and terror... a reminder of the barbaric practice by White people of lynching people of African ancestry in this country.

The school principal identified three White students that were responsible for the incident and recommended expulsion. [Police were not called even though this type of incident can reportedly be prosecuted as a federal hate crime.] The White superintendent of the school system overruled the principal and gave the students a routine in-school suspension. He went on to argue that the whole incident was just a foolish adolescent prank, suggesting that no harm or hurtful message was intended. In protest, it has been reported that a number of students organized a sit-in and continued to sit under the "White" tree. Numerous fights also reportedly occurred in the several days following.

On September 6, in an effort to end the protest and in response to the ongoing racial tensions in the school, the LaSalle Parish District Attorney was summoned to the school, accompanied by several police officers. At a school assembly, the DA reportedly threatened the protesting Black students by stating, "I can be your best friend or your worst enemy. I can take away your lives with the stroke of my pen."

On September 10, Black students attempted to address their concerns to the Jena school board. The school board refused to respond to their grievances, stating that the noose incident was just a prank and had already been responded to appropriately. Racial tensions remained high both at Jena High School and in Jena more generally throughout the fall semester.

November 2006: On Thursday, November 30, 2006 the main academic building of Jena High School was burned down. To date no charges have been filed, although the arson is believed to be connected with this racially charged series of events.

That weekend a Black student was repeatedly beaten up by several White males while he and several friends attempted to enter a predominantly White party. The White attackers were reported to have been local adults and not students. One White male was arrested and charged with battery several months after this incident. He received a sentence of probation.

Also that weekend, a White student pulled out a shotgun and threatened several Black students at a local convenience store. Fearing for their lives, the Black students took the gun away from the White student and ran away from the scene. The Black students were later charged with theft for taking the shotgun. No charges were filed against the White student that pulled the gun on the Black students.

The following Monday a White student who many recognized as being one of the most outspoken supporters of the students that hung the noose was reportedly beaten up by six Black students (the *Jena 6*). According to written accounts, a number of witnesses reported that the White student was taunting and harassing the Black student that had been beaten up by the White males during the prior weekend. According to witness accounts he also used the word "nigger" and/or other racial expletives while taunting the Black student. The White student was taken to the local hospital where he was treated for bruises and cuts to his face, and was released after a few hours. He attended a social function later that evening, where he was reportedly bragging to other White students about the incident.

Five of the six Black students were later arrested, expelled from school and charged (as adults) with assault. Their charges were later upgraded to second degree attempted murder. The sixth student was charged as a juvenile because he was 14 at the time of the incident.

Summer 2007 — Mychal Bell, the first of the six Black students to be tried in court, was found guilty of second degree battery and conspiracy to commit aggravated second degree battery by an all-White jury. It has been reported that some members of the jury had current and/or prior personal relationships with the White student that was roughed up and members of his family. Mychal Bell's public defender was very ineffective (some have argued so negligent as to constitute grounds for an appeal).

The charges against the Black students, and the subsequent conviction of Mychal Bell, sparked local and national outrage. A multi-racial coalition of individuals, organizations and radio personalities across the country have decried the overly punitive charges that are seen by many as far disproportional to the actual incident, as well as the fact that five of the six teens have been charged in adult court.

Mychal Bell was initially scheduled to be sentenced today, September 20, in Jena. On September 4, a judge dismissed the conspiracy charge against Mychal, but let stand the second degree attempted battery charge. He agreed, however, that he should never have been charged as an adult. Just last week (on September 14) an appeals court judge dismissed the remaining charge against Mychal, agreeing that Mychal should never have been charged as an adult. The DA vowed to appeal the appeals court ruling, taking the case to the Louisiana State Supreme Court.

Even with this ruling, however, Mychal can still be tried in juvenile court for his alleged role in the roughing-up of the White student. Meanwhile, the adult charges remain for the other four members of the *Jena 6.* Court proceedings are scheduled to begin for those youth in the near future. Meanwhile, bail has been rejected for Mychal Bell, and he remains locked up pending the resolution of the ongoing legal proceedings. He has been in jail for almost 10 months, into what would have been his senior year in high school.

A march and demonstration expected to attract more than 60,000 people from around the country is scheduled to take place today in Jena, Louisiana. Other rallies and protest marches are also being held today in cities around the country to draw attention to this horrible injustice. Much of the attention this series of incidents is receiving has been credited to national radio personalities, radio and television talk show hosts and other independent media institutions who have dedicated unprecedented air time to this issue and this tragic set of circumstances.

The *Jena 6* Story: A Critical Analysis

When Justice Fails — One of the many unfortunate things about this series of incidents in Jena is that it largely stemmed from a failure of formal leadership structures and legal institutions to respond in a just way to the criminal acts committed by these White youth and adults against the African American students at Jena High School. In the absence of justice, and in the presence of continued threats against their lives, these students appeared to resort to what some might argue was their only remaining option… self-defense. Had the appropriate actions been taken by the "authorities" *and the White youths' parents*, the ongoing intimidation and abuse of these African American students would potentially have been stopped much sooner. Interestingly, there has been little critical examination of the negligent role of "official" leadership and White parental responsibility in the face of these acts of racial terrorism. This is one of the many tragedies of this situation.

Corporate Mass Media — There are at least two ways the media can respond to the kinds of activities that have unfolded in Jena. They can either cover the story, or ignore it. Generally, the corporate media establishment decided to ignore it for almost a year. It wasn't until public awareness increased (largely as a result of independent media outlets and radio personalities) that the corporate mass media outlets began to cover the story in a more deliberate way.

Ironically, however, instead of providing a critical assessment of the history and context of the unfolding tragedy, the coverage seems to have focused exclusively on the outrage this tragedy has been creating around the world. The "story" for these corporate media institutions has largely been the national and international outcry, but *not* the series of clearly related and troubling incidents that sparked the outrage. To the extent the incidents themselves have been covered, it has frequently occurred as a way of juxtaposing the national outrage against the implied "law and order" rationale offered by the prosecution for their treatment of the *Jena 6.* There have been few exceptions to this pattern.

Also missing from this national corporate "mainstream" media coverage is a critical examination of the role the White students and adults have played in these incidents. It has largely been covered as a "Black" crime issue, as opposed to an issue also involving the clearly criminal and terrorizing behaviors of White youth and adults in Jena against the Black students.

The *Jena 6* Didn't Start This Mess! — As tragic as the circumstances are for the *Jena 6* students, it is important to point out that these dynamics started long before they were even born. The kinds of racist and criminal behaviors of these White adolescents are not a new phenomenon. Nor have these behaviors only recently re-emerged. Racial tensions have long existed in Jena, as with many other big and small cities and towns around this country. This is the legacy of White racism in the United States since the days of this country's founding. It may be the case that we don't hear about these incidents as often as we did in the past, but these incidents still happen all too frequently around the country. It remains a national disgrace and tragedy that the perpetrators of these types of racial terrorist acts rarely receive punishment comparable to their crimes.

The Big Picture: Racial Disparity in America's Juvenile Justice System

As I mentioned earlier, the experience of the *Jena 6* is typical in many ways of the kinds of experiences many of our young people have with this nation's juvenile and criminal justice systems. A brief review of national trends helps to illustrate this larger national tragedy and injustice.

In proportion to their presence in the nation's youth population, African American youth are far more likely than White youth to come into contact with the juvenile justice system. Generally, racial disparities tend to increase the further African American youth are processed through the system. The following statistics are taken from a January 2007 report entitled, *And Justice For Some: Differential Treatment of Youth of Color in the Justice System*:

From 2002 to 2004, African Americans were: 16% of this nation's youth population; 28% of juvenile arrests; 30% of referrals to juvenile court; 37% of the detained population; 34% of youth formally processed by the juvenile court; 30% of adjudicated youth (cases resolved without further punitive involvement); 35% of youth judicially waived to criminal court (charged as adults); 38% of youth in residential placement; and 58% of youth admitted to state adult prison. At each of the critical decision-making stages of this nation's juvenile and criminal justice systems, African American youth are treated more punitively than their White counterparts.

Our Challenge Moving Forward: Acting Now With a Long-Term Vision

One challenge for the current generation of young people is for us to work tirelessly to ensure that we don't pass these pathological patterns of racism and injustice on to our children and grandchildren. It may be the case that racism will continue to exist. But we do not have to accept these inhumane and unjust societal arrangements. In the words of Frantz Fanon, in his classic work *Wretched of the Earth*, "each generation, out of relative obscurity, must define its mission, fulfill it, or betray it." The kind of injustice we see in Jena today is but one of many challenges that are before us. We can each commit to fighting against this injustice or sit on the sideline while others step up in our place.

<u>We Stand On Solid Ground</u> — Many people complain that we have lost a generation or two of young people that are disengaged from the struggle against racism. Yet there are frequently ebbs and flows to social justice movements. While this is true, it is also worth noting that the struggle for racial justice in this country never ceased. There have always been individuals and organizations working on the front lines of the struggle against racism and cultural hegemony in this country. We owe a debt of appreciation and gratitude for their sacrifices and their ongoing efforts to keep "waving the flag" and "beating the drums" of justice and resistance.

We still know enough about the history of our ancestors in this country to know what forms the struggle has taken, and what the struggle has produced. More importantly, we can still study and learn from our elders and ancestors so that we can be wiser in our efforts. As Malcolm X stated, "of all our studies, *history* is best qualified to reward our research; for the future belongs to those who prepare for it today."

The Way Forward — Our challenge is clear. We hold the power and the potential to change this nation. *Jena 6* highlights just a few of the contours and complexities of the enduring challenges facing African American families and communities trying to make it this country. While there are indeed many "issues" and challenges facing the African American community, it does not mean that we should not focus on this one. We have an obligation to resist, challenge and confront injustice in all of its forms. This is clearly one of those forms.

I appreciate and commend the individuals and organizations that have stepped up to make all of us more aware of the *Jena 6* incidents as they have unfolded for more than a year now. As we can see, when people have access to clearly articulated information about injustice, they tend to respond. It is up to all of us to continue to shine a light on this and other injustices we come across… and there are many!

It is encouraging to see what appears to be an awakened consciousness of at least one of the ways in which racism and injustice have taken form over the last several decades. While I celebrate what appears to be an increased sense of outrage, energy and activism, I encourage us all to keep our focus sharp and our stamina up, as there is a great deal more injustice that we have to simultaneously turn our attention to. *Aluta Continua! (The struggle continues!)*

Ten

Stephen Biko and the South African Black Consciousness Movement: Implications for African American Family Well-Being

November 12, 2007

"...there are lessons to be learned by all of us as we endeavor to address the over-involvement of African American children and families in this nation's child welfare and juvenile justice systems."

Earlier this year (January 17) I wrote an essay reflecting on the life and legacy of Dr. Martin Luther King, Jr. This current essay is similarly the result of my reflections on another great international leader and activist, Stephen Biko.

As described in the book, *I Write What I Like*, "Steve Biko died in 1977 at the age of thirty from a head wound suffered while in the custody of police. For his steadfast refusal to keep quiet about the heinous crimes of apartheid, he is honored as the martyred hero of the South African liberation movement."

Steve Biko became known by many outside of South Africa because of the reason and manner of his death. He was very active in, and credited by many as being the father of, South Africa's Black Consciousness Movement. September 12, 2007 marked the 30th anniversary of Steve Biko's brutal murder while in police detention in South Africa.

Like Dr. King's birthday, I often spend time around this date every year reading through some of Steve Biko's writings and speeches, and reflecting on the significance of his life and legacy. This year, in addition to online accounts of his speeches and work, I primarily found myself re-reading his writings in the classic book, *I Write What I Like.* While reading Biko's words, I most often found myself drawing parallels between his analysis of the struggle against apartheid in South Africa and our ongoing struggles against racism and other forms of oppression in this country.

My intent in this essay, however, is not only to draw parallels between apartheid in South Africa and the African American experience. Others have done so quite effectively. What I would like to do is reflect on Steve Biko's analysis of the South African condition under the apartheid system, the importance of Black Consciousness, and how he thus approached his organizing and community development work aimed at the healing and liberation of the people. Within his ideas I believe there are lessons to be learned by all of us as we endeavor to address the over-involvement of African American children and families in this nation's child welfare and juvenile justice systems.

Ultimately, Steve Biko dedicated his life to operationalizing a paradigm that sought to heal and liberate African people (and through that all people in South Africa) from the effects of European colonization and the dangerous myth of White supremacy. It is in his life's work that we can find meaningful lessons.

Let me share at the outset an organizational note for this essay. In several sections I will use quotes from Steve Biko's book *I Write What I Like* to set up or highlight a particular idea or reflection. Where you see references to page numbers, these are page numbers where the quote can be found in the book.

Understanding Black Consciousness

I would like to begin by defining Black Consciousness. I will do so by sharing statements from Steve Biko about Black Consciousness and its relevance to the healing and liberation of African people living under the Apartheid system in South Africa. In these statements I believe we can find direct parallels to the challenges facing us in our continued support of African American families and communities struggling through our involvement with this nation's child welfare and juvenile justice systems. Each of the italicized excerpts is from the book, *I Write What I Like.*

Defining Black Consciousness

Let us begin by defining Black Consciousness. At risk of over-simplifying a more complex idea and philosophical perspective, I will use a brief excerpt of a definition offered by Steve Biko. I do so fully aware that many African Americans have offered similar definitions and analyses of Black Consciousness, especially as it relates to the African American experience.

On page 49, Biko describes Black Consciousness as: *"the realisation by the Black man of the need to rally together with his brothers… and to operate as a group in order to rid themselves of the shackles that bind them to perpetual servitude. It seeks to demonstrate the lie that Black is an aberration from the "normal" which is white. It is a manifestation of a new realization that by seeking to run away from themselves and to emulate the white man, blacks are insulting the intelligence of whoever created them black. Black consciousness therefore takes cognizance of the deliberateness of God's plan in creating Black people Black. It seeks to infuse the Black community with a new-found pride in themselves, their efforts, their values systems, their culture, their religion and their outlook on life."*

As may be obvious, Biko's analysis of Black Consciousness exists as a response to the history of European

/ White cultural, political, and economic hegemony in South Africa. It can be argued that in the absence of European / White (and other) interference African people, and thus African culture and institutional structures, would exist in their own right. Black Consciousness affirms the integrity and value of the African "way" in the presence of oppressive and anti-African people and influences.

As Biko argues, Black Consciousness is not a means towards an end per se. It is a way of being, feeling and thinking that affirms the integrity of the African experience and cultural meaning system. It is a framework through which Black people accept the beauty and value in our experiences and culture, and through such, endeavor to create societal structures, institutions and communities that promote the well-being and optimal growth and development of African people... as *we* come to understand and define it.

Any effort on our part to learn from and adopt aspects of the cultural values and technologies of non-Black peoples must be done on our terms and for the purposes of the continued growth and development of Black families and communities.

Understanding the Black Condition

As mentioned previously, Biko was sharply criticized by Whites for his analysis and activism. Not only did many of them disagree with his assertion that African people have a culture that is (at the very least) equal in value to European /

White culture, they saw his assertions and activism as a direct threat to their continued hegemony in southern Africa. Their ruling structure and oppressive regime after all was based on the premise (although unfounded) of European / White supremacy in relation to all other peoples.

For his views Biko was frequently detained and brought up on various legal charges. The following analysis was shared by Steve Biko while under cross-examination in a South African court during the first week of May 1976. A number of Black Consciousness leaders were being tried, fundamentally, because of their involvement in spreading views associated with Black Consciousness.

In the following excerpt (from page 114), Biko describes for the court the fundamental goals of "conscientizing" Black people as bringing a stronger consciousness of the integrity, honor and empowering potential of Black people's history and culture:

"This is correct, we do make references to the conditions of the black man and the conditions in which the black man lives. We try to get blacks in conscientisation to grapple realistically with their problems, to attempt to find solutions to their problems, to develop what one might call an awareness, a physical awareness of their situation, to be able to analyse it, and to provide answers for themselves. The purpose behind it really being to provide some kind of hope; I think the central theme about black society is that it has got elements of a defeated society, people often look like they have given up the struggle. Like the man who was telling me that he now lives to work, he has given himself to the idea. Now this

sense of defeat is basically what we are fighting against; people must not just give in to the hardship of life, people must develop a hope, people must develop some form of security to be together to look at their problems, and people must in this way build up their humanity. This is the point about conscientisation and Black Consciousness."

A key message in this text is the notion that people must find the hope and strength to persevere through the process of grappling with and understanding the complexities of our condition. This is a collective process, as people come to understand their condition through critical examination. This is a learning and discovery process at its core, and comes through critical inquiry and analysis… alongside other individuals experiencing similar conditions.

This suggests that a critical activity for adults and youth struggling through life's predicaments must be a critical examination of their circumstance within the context of our historical / cultural experiences in this country. For our purposes in this country, this critical examination must place the substance of the African American experience in this larger society and within the community at the center. Ideally, people must grapple with the meaning of their experiences *together*, and develop shared understandings and collective working solutions as we sort through the challenges presented. This is fundamentally an evolving *meaning-seeking* exercise, and requires constant engagement.

It could appear at face value that many people today are disillusioned at the current state of the African American community. It is certainly possible for people to look at popular depictions of African American families and communities found in the mass media and conclude that we are complacent and no longer committed to any form of struggle. It could appear to many that we have come to accept our condition as being natural, justified, and/or "just the way it is."

Similar observations and misunderstandings existed in South African society, even during the brutal and unjust years of the apartheid system. In the following excerpt, Biko argues against this observation as being short-sighted and just scratching the surface:

"That is I think understating the position. I think it is possible to adapt to a given hard situation precisely because you have got to live it, and you have got to live with it every day. But adapting does not mean that you forget; you go to the mill every day, it is always unacceptable to you, it has always been unacceptable to you, and it remains so for life, but you adapt in the sense that you cannot continue to live in a state of conflict with yourself. You sort of accept, like the man who was working with the electrician was saying to me, you know, 'oh he talks this way'. This is his explanation of it. This is his sort of glib adaptation to it, but deep inside him he feels it. He cannot keep on answering back to him every day: don't call me boy, don't shout at me, don't swear at me, because there is also the element of the job that he has got to keep. He had adapted but he does not forget it, and he does not accept it, which I think is important."

This is a critical point for us to consider and reflect on because we see signs of adaptation to oppression all around us. These appearances can be, and often are, confused with signs of defeatism. Many families are forced to live in neighborhoods riddled with crime, substance abuse, sexual abuse, substandard housing, inferior educational opportunities, environmental pollution, police brutality and other pathologies. While families frequently reject these conditions and behaviors as unacceptable, we tend to find ways to adapt in the interest of *getting by* and avoiding what are too frequently negative repercussions and retaliation.

The same applies to the subtle and more explicit forms of racism African American people encounter daily. We do not accept any of it per se. We are clear that it is denigrating and disrespectful. Yet we often find ourselves silent (or *silenced*) in the interest of "getting by," keeping our job, avoiding physical confrontations, etc. Paul Lawrence Dunbar describes our reality very clearly in his poem: *We wear the mask*.

Let us also not forget or minimize the strong sense of fear and insecurity felt by many African Americans as a result of the experiences of individuals and organizations that dare to speak out and organize actively against the status quo. Freedom is not free, and as history teaches us, the price can be costly.

Meanwhile and on a deeper level, if you really watch the daily lifestyle patterns, routines and behaviors of some segments of our community, you can see very clear signs of fatigue and depression when it comes to any form of meaningful struggle against oppression. As I mentioned earlier, I do not believe we have become a lifeless and lethargic people. To the contrary, we continue to be among the most expressive and culturally rich peoples in the world. What I am saying is that a great number of black folks have adopted lifestyles that allow us to "get by" and preserve some sense of sanity and energy to make it through each day (e.g. "living for the weekend").

Too often, unfortunately, this is a lifestyle devoid of any critical examination of our individual and collective condition. It is a lifestyle devoid of any real and meaningful "us-centered" institution-building activity. It is thus a lifestyle that keeps us disconnected from one another when it comes to identifying and developing workable solutions to the challenges facing our families and communities.

This is why the punitive child welfare and juvenile justice systems (among other systems) can come into our communities, with no meaningful resistance from us, and fill a void of problem-solving for our so-called "at-risk" families and youth. There is a great deal for us to learn from Fannie Lou Hamer about what it means to be "*sick and tired of being sick and tired.*"

Toward a Critical Analysis

The child welfare community in this country has yet to fully acknowledge the historical foundations (ideas, values, etc.) upon which this nation's child welfare system was built, and how that foundation has contributed (and continues to) to the state of affairs we refer to as racial disproportionality and disparate outcomes in child welfare. The same can be said for juvenile justice in this country, although some steps have been taken to force jurisdictions around the country to critically explore and address these dynamics.

The Substance of a Collective Critical Analysis

I believe there are a few critical questions we must reflect on, within a framework of Black Consciousness and with a sense of urgency, as we continue our efforts to bring our children and families home from and out of the clutches of the punitive child welfare and juvenile justice systems:

1) What does our history and culture tell us about what it means to be "well?" 2) What would optimal health and wellness look like for African American children and families in today's society? 3) What is it about the African American experience that has rendered so many of our families vulnerable to the challenges we find ourselves facing? 4) What can we learn from prior generations of African American families and communities about family and community well-being? 5) What resources are necessary to heal and realize the

optimal development of African American families and the broader African American community? 6) What can each of us do as individuals, but working collectively, to secure and make strategic use of these resources so that our families and communities become well? 7) What must each of us *stop* doing in order for us to realize optimal African American family and community well-being? 8) What is it about America's human services and juvenile/criminal justice institutions that has made them historically oppressive in their relationship to the broader African American community? 9) What strategies can we employ to reverse this historic pattern?

If we can respond to the above questions effectively, keeping in mind the observations and reflections offered by Steve Biko, we would find ourselves well on our way to healing our families in a way we have yet to realize. I don't assume that these are new ideas. I am also fully aware that many individuals and organizations have grappled with different variations of these questions repeatedly during our many years in this country. Revisiting these prior conversations, speeches, writings and efforts is a natural starting point.

The Context of a Collective Critical Analysis

What does/would a collective critical analysis process look like? You don't have to look hard to find examples; nor is it difficult to create the space for these efforts (both in informal settings as well as in more formal institutional settings). The seeds for this kind of critical analysis process and collective organizing work exists informally in many places. For example, go to a typical barber shop after a Black athlete, entertainer or politician gets in trouble with the law. You will see Black folks talking about what these individuals should have done differently, as well as how unjust society is when it comes to Black people and interests. You see some of this play out in the more progressive churches, other religious institutions and some civic organizations as well.

Most of us have our opinions about what we feel is an American society that is racist and unjust at its core. The problem is that most of us do not belong to, or are otherwise disconnected from, organizations that engage in this kind of analysis and social justice work every day.

I am arguing that we need more structured and deliberate spaces and opportunities to have these conversations. We have the physical places and mechanisms to do so. They include: our schools, colleges and universities; our local community centers; our neighborhood and other civic organizations; our fraternities and sororities; our professional organizations; as well as our local parent teacher associations. What we have to do is create more deliberate and dedicated time and space in these various settings for these serious conversations and the community building strategy development work.

What could these programs look like? There are various forms that these critical consciousness-raising efforts can take.

We need more non-fiction book clubs that function more like study groups, and fewer that spend great deals of time reading the lusty fiction novels that are ever more present in our community. I suspect that will offend many people. So be it… our ancestors and future generations deserve better. We need more movie viewing and discussion groups that critically analyze the images of African and African American individuals, families and communities displayed on the screen. These groups must be organized and prepared to speak and write about their observations and critical findings. We need Saturday Schools, Weekend Academies and after school programs that are explicitly dedicated to the mental, spiritual, and physical development of our children and families, and with a lens of Black Consciousness and social justice. We need more churches and other organizations to host lecture series and cultural studies groups that provide a critical focus our communities' challenges.

The outcome of all of these activities should be a clear analysis of who we are, where we have been and where we are going. It must also be a goal of ours to develop the institutions and resources needed to meet the needs of our children, families and communities. There must be no dichotomy between the social justice advocacy and other self-help activities of our organizations. Both have been a strong part of our community tradition in this country, and must be reclaimed as a part of our organizing efforts moving forward.

There are examples of all of these efforts in existence. We need much more of it.

Is Our Goal Systems Reform or Transformation?

Many people have raised the question of whether we are involved in societal and systems reform efforts, or more fundamental societal and systems transformation efforts. On page 49, Biko argues that the aim of the Black Consciousness movement was not to reform the system, but to completely transform it. Reform, according to Biko, implies "an acceptance of the major points around which the system revolves."

The same is true, from my perspective, of the systems of child welfare and juvenile justice in America. The basic values and principles undergirding current practice and policy in these fields is contrary to culturally responsive principles of child, family and community development and well-being. Thus, we seek to redefine the fundamental functions of the child welfare and juvenile justice systems. It is true that some efforts are and have been underway to do so in this country; however, to date those efforts have not reached a critical mass.

Concluding Thoughts

I have offered the ideas presented in this essay as a way to stimulate more critical thinking about how we approach our work in education, child welfare, juvenile justice and broader youth and family development. We must approach our work from a perspective rooted in a substantive analysis of our historical and cultural experiences in this country. It must be centered in a framework of Black (African) Consciousness.

One of the key messages and examples Steve Biko shared with us is that our power and our strength comes from our *collective* critical examination of and attention to these dynamics. The natural product of such critical examination is the identification of the working solutions to our challenges, and the collective courage and commitment to: a) start right now, and b) start where we find ourselves.

We have the ability and resources, right now, to address the major challenges that face African American youth, families and communities. What we need is an institutional infrastructure to support it. As I have mentioned a number of times before… We can do this! And we can do this in our lifetime!

Let us commit ourselves to doing what we must to heal and rebuild our families and communities! Let us *stop* doing those things that distract us and stand in our way! Our children, and those yet unborn, are depending on us. We have a lot of work to do!

Eleven

One Person's Testimony: Rediscovering and reclaiming your voice during life's most difficult days

December 5, 2008

"Compassion, with a deep appreciation of the challenges, pain and suffering of other people, can help free us up to experience our own healing. But we have to be present enough to focus on others and not just our own challenges, pain and suffering."

I'll share at the outset that writing this essay has been a very different experience for me, compared to the others I have written. This has, by far, been the most difficult essay for me to write. I hope it has even a fraction of the meaning for some of you that it has had for me while writing it.

My Testimony

In this essay, I want to reflect on some dynamics I have been experiencing, at least in a more pronounced way, for the last year or more. I am clear that some of my motive for sharing these experiences is probably selfish. I am certainly hoping that writing about these dynamics helps to free my spirit up a bit. But more so, I hope that reading this essay will help some of you reflect on and perhaps appreciate the need for us to heal ourselves, our families, and to reach out to those individuals we know are struggling... helping to find that peace that we all seek. We are the only ones we've got, so we've got to pull it together.

Cancer

The last year has been extremely challenging for me. I have found myself at so many different extremes of life's emotional spectrum. As many of you know my brother, Khari Miller, has been battling cancer for almost nine years. He was diagnosed with Hodgkin's Lymphoma in March of 2000. He has fought valiantly thus far and continues to fight the good fight. The cancer is still present, and continues to spread, but slow enough for Khari to keep living a life of passion, meaning and purpose. I know it's been extremely difficult for him; and I also know it's been difficult for others close to him, including myself.

Doctors have called Khari a walking and living miracle, precisely because of how extensively the cancer had spread throughout his body by the time he was diagnosed. The first oncologists that took his case gave him a maximum six months to live, even with the initial advanced chemotherapy and radiation treatments they were prescribing. Within the last eight years he's been through multiple regimens of chemotherapy and radiation treatments and several experimental cancer treatments. He has also undergone two bone marrow / stem cell transplants, for which I had the honor of being the donor. I am so thankful that he is still with us, and continues to press on.

Relatively recently, I found out that two other individuals that I am close to were diagnosed with cancer. In early 2008 my father was diagnosed with early stages of prostate cancer. After several months of consultation with multiple doctors and a number of prostate cancer survivors, as well as months of careful research and consideration, my father decided to undergo a newly developed laser surgery to have the cancer removed. I am so thankful to report that the surgery was very successful. As far as we know, this was by far a best case scenario for the family.

Also last spring another very close friend and colleague was diagnosed with a challenging case of breast cancer. This past summer she underwent a pair of surgeries, and now continues to undergo regular chemotherapy treatments. She is hanging in there as well, but it continues to be very challenging.

While each of these individuals is very close to my heart, it's been difficult being completely responsive to each of them and their respective challenges with an open and prayerful heart.

Closer to Home

During this same time period my relationship with another individual, who has certainly been closest to my heart for the past almost ten years, has unraveled at the seams, seemingly at record speed. This particular experience, which really escalated last spring, has been most difficult to cope with and make sense of.

I always thought I was at peace with, or at least in control of, my emotions and reflections on my foster care and adoption experience. I can say very clearly now that this recent and still unfolding experience has evoked some of the most painful and frightening feelings of rejection and abandonment that I have ever been forced to deal with. This experience has exposed many feelings and emotions I honestly never knew existed within me. This experience has touched the core of who I am, spiritually and emotionally, and has challenged many of my assumptions about relationships , marriage and family.

During the last nine months I have experienced very concerning night sweats and other body temperature fluctuations, heaviest during the summer and early fall. I simultaneously lost approximately 15-20 pounds. It's been a rough period, with many highs and lows, moments of hope and despair, as well as some periods of extreme anger, resentment and frustration. Fortunately, I can now see a light of hope and healing off in the distance, and I continue to work through this experience anxiously and prayerfully.

Why am I sharing this?

Now why am I sharing all of this, and particularly in this format? Like I said earlier I am sure some of this is selfish. Writing is a healing exercise for me. Writing is my outlet for personal reflection and expression. Just writing about some of these experiences and dynamics helps me feel better… just getting it off my chest. Acknowledging the pain is liberating.

Moreover, I grew up within the Black church tradition. A big part of that tradition is expressiveness, evidenced in the tradition of testifying. Testifying serves many different purposes. Sometimes we testify because we know what we've been through, and we just want to give thanks to the Creator for guiding us through it. Sometimes we testify because what we are going through still hurts, and we just need to acknowledge it so that we can work through it.

I recognize that the totality of my recent experiences has pushed me way past my old comfort zone and has forced me to deal with things that are so painful… fear of being alone, rejection, abandonment and loss; a rigidity in my core values and sensibilities; and very sharp perspectives on the importance of family, relationships and marriage. I wanted to reflect openly on at least some of this, so that maybe even just one other person can benefit from my experience and perhaps find a more peaceful and healing space to live in. This is exactly what I am trying to do right now.

Being Open to Possibilities

For much of my adult life I have frowned on the typical American approach toward therapy and counseling in this "not well" society of ours. I always frowned on it as being culturally out of sync and detached. For the most part I still fundamentally believe that is true about the field. In the last several months, however, I have actually opened myself up to the possible benefits of seeing a counselor. It's been a productive experience so far. I was afraid for the longest time because all of the people that I knew (among my peers) that had undergone marriage counseling had ended up in a personal space and place that I was afraid of being in. But I was desperate to talk with someone and wanted affirmation that I wasn't going crazy in my reactions to some of the dynamics I was struggling to make sense of.

I'm still very much in the midst of it, but I want to acknowledge that I was a little off base in my assessment. Counseling is certainly not *the answer* to the problems we face, but it can be a powerful resource and process for helping us make sense of what we are experiencing. Indeed I still believe the counselor needs to be culturally in sync with you, but if that is the case it can be a powerful experience. It has been and continues to be for me. It really has helped me make sense of my current circumstances, and it has also pushed me to work on and work through some of the understandable - yet still unhealthy - aspects of my personality.

I have also come to appreciate some other things as of late. The first is the important reminder that I have been and continue to be blessed beyond measure… "blessed and highly favored" as we tend to say.

I have certainly been directly affected by the experiences of my close friends and family members battling cancer. I am also clear that I am not the one that has to endure the difficult physical challenges presented by surgery, chemotherapy and radiation. Sure it hurts personally to see loved ones struggling against illnesses as serious as these, but the ordeal they experience is very different. When it's all said and done, however, all of us share a mutual responsibility to be a support and healing resource for one another along this journey. And let's be clear that we cannot help others if we are not at least half-way well ourselves. Compassion, with a deep appreciation of the challenges, pain and suffering of other people, can help free us up to experience our own healing. But we have to be present enough to focus on others and not just our own challenges, pain and suffering.

In talking with some of my close friends I have come to appreciate that when we are struggling through depression or some other life challenges, we are not the only ones affected. As I have tried to work through these challenges in recent months, I have hurt others that are close to me. My style is to retreat and close myself off to others when things get hard. I can even lash out at others that try to get close enough to help. That only creates more pain and hurt for the very people that are closest to us and care about us. It also disconnects us from the real healing work and relationships we have been put in this world to nurture and develop. I am more clear now that the only way we can get through some of our "stuff" is to deal with it straight up and out in the open. To work through it with the very people that are closest to us and care most about us is critical.

What does this all mean?

Now let me tie this together in some kind of coherent way. As I mentioned, writing this essay has been a bit more challenging for me than usual. I also realize that what I am sharing in this essay accounts for why I haven't even written an essay in over a year. It explains why I have only half-heartedly pursued those relationships, ideas, activities and life goals that are most fulfilling for me. It explains why I haven't given more of myself to the individuals closest to me.

This, brothers and sisters, isn't truly living. Unfortunately, however, this is the way many of us walk along life's path. No longer will this be my story. I appreciate now, more than ever, that my children deserve to see their father live life with the passion, enthusiasm, courage, and determination that the Creator has blessed me with. I have to be the example they came into this world to learn from. I have my family and my closest friends to thank for helping me realize and appreciate this.

Deep depression and the pain and stress of dealing with life's profound challenges can be paralyzing if we aren't careful. That has been my reality for the last year directly, and for a number of years more generally. I am much more clear about it now, however. I hope some of these reflections will help me, as well as some of you, or others you are close to, think more reflectively about how to respond to these kinds of life dynamics.

African American Men and Fathers

I don't know many (or any) African American men that are fully open and honest about their feelings, fears insecurities and personal struggles. I have seen too many of us suffer as a result. I have seen both directly and indirectly the painful and costly impact of suicide, unnatural disease, premature death, depression, rage, anger and frustration on our families and our community. Contrary to popular perceptions presented in the media or in the "professional literature," I believe so much of this comes not from a lack of care, concern, compassion and love for our families and community, but precisely an inability to show that care, concern, compassion and love in ways that feel welcomed and affirming.

I would like to add my voice to the chorus of African American men and women, past and present, that have cried out for African American men to wake up and reconnect with who we truly are. We have a lot to say, a lot of stories to tell, and a lot of work to do. We have to find healthy and consistent strategies for opening up and giving of ourselves... ways that are productive yet different from what we are used to, and perhaps even painful in the moment. I can tell you, though, that we *can* get through it. We have to get through it. Our families and communities are depending on us. We must to do better. I know what some of the challenges are. I also know, as do many of you, what some of the possibilities are. African American fathers, husbands, brothers, sons, cousins, uncles and grandfathers we have to get it together.

African American mothers, wives, sisters, daughters, cousins, aunts and grandmothers please find ways to open up the space and place in your hearts for African American men to be what is healthy and natural and necessary. Those of you who are able, teach other young girls and ladies how to do the same. We must continue to learn with and from one another. We are complimentary, and can only do this together. Indeed, there are some relationships that might not work in the immediate sense, but we must still be respectful, loving and compassionate as we create a healthy, life affirming and healing space within which we can interact… and our children can develop.

Our Charge

We have to want a healthy and whole community as badly as our ancestors did. Indeed, we've got a lot of work to do. But we can do it, and we can do it in our lifetime. From this moment forward, I ask that you also reflect on what it means to be well, to be present and to be compassionate. Develop strategies in your own life to make this a reality. Reclaim your voice as you continue to walk along life's path. Speak with courage and conviction, and most importantly through your conduct and your example.

We are our only saviors. We are the legacy of our ancestors. We are the examples for our children. We are the hope of our future generations… our children yet unborn. It's healing time!

Twelve

Reflections on Another Child Fatality: We Must Do Better By Our Children

January 7, 2009

"Next time you find yourself making pronouncements about how things need to be done differently with these systems... finish your statement with the following words: '...and I will take the first step to make it happen.'"

I need to be completely honest as I start this essay. I haven't always had much sympathy for or a solid understanding of the trials and tribulations of social workers working in public child welfare agencies. My introduction to public child welfare was really through the experiences of African American adoption agencies, many of which have endured their own share of struggles partnering with these large bureaucratic and frequently culturally unresponsive systems. I guess it's also safe to say that some of my initial perceptions and perspective was based on my own personal experience with public child welfare systems.

My birth mother was pressured to give my brother and me up for adoption, during pregnancy and up until birth. After being placed voluntarily by our birth mother, our birth father and his family were turned away from the public child welfare agency after attempting to get my brother and me out of foster care. All of this I am sure contributed to my lack of compassion for and appreciation of the struggles of these systems, as well as the individuals working within them. As far as I was concerned they were the heartless and oppressive enemy – tearing African American families apart with no care or concern.

In my current job I am responsible for working directly with public child welfare agencies to achieve better outcomes for children and families, specifically providing support and technical assistance for their system improvement efforts. Whereas I once critiqued the work of these agencies looking in from the outside, I am now responsible for supporting the system transformation efforts they are all engaged in. Now critiquing from a distance isn't an option. I have to be a part of the solution or be out. How interesting, given my own personal experience and previous perspective.

In my professional work over the last several years I have had an opportunity to work closely with social workers and child welfare administrators as they have attempted to transform their child welfare systems. In doing so I have gained a much greater appreciation for what individuals working within these systems struggle through and against every day. These are large and complex bureaucratic systems. As a parent of two wonderful children I can assure you that actually caring for children is easy compared to transforming these huge systems. At no time do I have a greater appreciation of these dynamics more than when a child dies.

A few years ago I was involved in an on-going project working directly with child welfare administrators, social workers, community partners, as well as youth and birth parents that were themselves once involved with the child welfare system. During that period one of the state systems we were working with experienced a child fatality. A young child had been removed from her family and placed in foster care. After a short period of time in care, the young girl was reunified with her family. She was killed within weeks of being reunified.

Everyone involved with this child's case was in strong agreement about returning this child home to her parents. When they heard the child had been killed by the step-father, everyone was devastated. To ensure their safety, the remaining siblings were immediately removed from the home and placed in foster care. The media raked the agency over the coals about the tragedy, calling for accountability, independent investigations and massive agency reforms, all the while demanding that the workers and administrators be fired.

I followed the media reports closely while also talking with the staff and administrators about some of the dynamics surrounding the incident. A supervisor shared with me the daily struggles they were trying to get through as the media continued to pile it on. She described to me the general fear they live with on a daily basis, knowing that every decision they make could be one that either supports the child's continued positive growth and development or puts the child in harm's way. She talked about hearing the media reports during that evening the news broke, praying that the accused family and the child that was murdered wasn't one they had worked with. She described the gut-wrenching feeling that came over her when she got the call shortly after seeing the media reports, confirming her worst fears. She tried to describe the harrowing feeling, like the life had been sucked out of her, when she found out who the girl was. She and the administrator both tried to describe this scenario repeatedly but couldn't get through it without breaking down and crying.

Later, this same supervisor talked about how challenging it was to explain to the remaining children what happened to their little sister. She talked about how hard it was to explain to them why they were taken away from their parents and why they were not allowed to see them. She talked about how hard it was to get the siblings to go to school and continue with their daily routines. She talked about how hard it was to get the siblings ready for the funeral services, with reporters and cameras everywhere. She talked about how she hadn't been able to sleep at night since finding out about the child's death. She talked about the relentless pressure placed on her to fire the social worker that was the primary case manager.

It was a very lonely and stressful period for her as well as all of the other staff and administrators connected with this child and her family. Everyone outside seemingly wanted to place blame and no one wanted to believe that the agency really did do "everything right." As tragic as the fatality was, the system seemingly could not have done anything more appropriate given the specific dynamics that played out with the family.

Having been involved on this side of the child welfare system, it's difficult to read and hear the news stories talking about most child fatalities. None of the reporters are present when the social workers have to tell a child's birth parents, or family of origin, that their child has died. The reporters aren't present when the social workers explain to a child's siblings that their brother or sister has died, and that they won't ever be able to see them or talk with them again. They aren't there when all the social worker can do is hold and embrace the child for hours at night until they either fall asleep or stop crying. The reporters aren't present when the social workers stay up at night responding to the children's nightmares, post-traumatic stress and depression. The reporters aren't present when the social workers help the children get dressed and ready to attend the funeral services. They weren't there during the weeks following the funeral services when the social workers had to continue explaining to the children what it all meant.

The reporters must not know that the social workers and administrators also have to live the rest of their lives wondering if the child might still be alive if only they did just one thing differently… if only they made one different decision. No one talks about the social workers and their grieving process. No one reports on the social workers who quit their jobs and refuse to ever work again as a child welfare social worker because of the guilt and fear that they might "kill another child."

The reporters don't talk about this side of the work. For that matter, many city and state elected officials also don't know about or appreciate these dynamics related to a child fatality when they make their pronouncements in front of the media about investigations, accountability and the firing of staff and administrators.

After learning of a pair of child fatalities several months ago in Maryland and the initial reporting about this horrific tragedy, I could not help but write this essay as a tribute to all social workers who give it their all every day and every night… all of those social workers that wake up every day praying that "their children" are alright… praying every day that none of their children's cases make the headlines.

I also cannot help but think about the reality that so many more children come into foster care because social workers, supervisors, administrators and even judges don't want to risk being wrong about a family. There are also the many "non-traditional" or "non-ideal" families and relatives that would be wonderful adoptive and kinship families but don't make it through the licensing process because of the agency's fear that something might happen. So many more children end up staying in foster care so much longer because of the public's perception of child welfare, largely influenced by the media and the all-too-frequent knee-jerk reactions of elected officials.

So the next time you see a horrific tragedy involving children somehow connected to this nation's child welfare system please withhold judgment until all of the facts come out. Be willing to accept that you may never know all of the facts surrounding the case. Assume for a change that the child welfare system may have done everything it could have, given its attempt to balance its mission of supporting families, protecting children from harm and respecting the rights of families to care for their children without unreasonable and unjustifiable intrusion from "state systems."

I will be the first to say that child welfare systems do too often tear families apart unfairly and unnecessarily, fail to provide supports that meet their basic needs and fail to provide optimal living arrangements for children when they must be removed from their families of origin. I am also clear that these very systems too frequently place children in settings that are no better - or even worse - than the settings they were removed from. I will also be the first to say that as individual citizens we know so little about how these systems work, and that our failure to understand these systems actually contributes to their ineffectiveness.

So the next time you find yourself heartbroken or even getting outraged about a child fatality, get inspired and get involved. Volunteering is always fine, but I am talking about really getting involved in their system transformation efforts. Organize community coalitions that partner with systems to achieve better outcomes for families and children, as opposed to only critiquing from a distance. There is a time for criticism, but it has to be followed by active and persistent efforts to achieve meaningful improvements.

Discover your role as a "regular citizen" in creating safety nets so that struggling families have a place to turn. Reach out to your neighbors and develop relationships so that our children don't go unnoticed for months or years before we find out something has gone horribly wrong. Stop complaining about paying taxes to support ineffective and frequently under-resourced bureaucratic systems and actually help to take the stress and weight off of these systems.

We *can* transform this nation's child welfare system. Indeed, we *must*! In their current form, many of these local systems don't adequately meet even the basic support needs of our families and children. They do need to be held accountable. But we all have to stop offering our armchair critiques and get involved. There are many talented and committed people working within these systems and supporting children and families. Whether we individually like it or not, these systems have the power and legal mandate to intervene when they suspect that children have been or may be maltreated. If you don't like how they do it, my challenge to you is to do your part to transform these systems into what they truly can and should be.

These are our families and our children. We have got to step up! Next time you find yourself making pronouncements about how things need to be different with these systems... finish your statement with the following words: *"...and I will take the first step to make it happen."* We have everything we need to transform our community and make all of our families stronger. We can do this in our lifetime. Let's start right now. We have a lot of work to do!

Thirteen

Toward a Healing Vision for Child Welfare Practice

April 10, 2009

"While we don't frequently talk about our work in such terms, so much of our work is really about supporting the 'healing' and development of families and family systems, especially when a family's challenges are perceived to pose a threat to the well-being of children."

Several weeks ago I traveled home to Detroit for a few days. A close relative was having surgery to remove a tumor found on a kidney. On the morning of the surgery I hung around the house for a few hours to join a conference call for work, and then prepared to go over to the hospital for the remainder of the day.

As I started to get ready I began to think about my relative, who I was told by phone had just begun the actual surgical procedure. As I continued to get ready I couldn't help but visualize what must have been going on in the operating room, and the nuances of the actual procedure. As one might assume, I was certainly reflective and prayerful in those moments, clear about the potential risk of any surgery that attempts to remove a portion of an internal organ. The more I thought about the procedure and the process, the more my thoughts drifted to thinking about the surgical team (the surgeon as well as the other people in the room working to ensure a successful outcome). I had an image in my head of concentration, clarity of focus and teamwork.

As I started to drive over to the hospital I started to think more and more about the fact that, as I was very much focused on the seriousness of what was happening with a family member, everyone around (naturally) continued to go about their own business. As I continued, I wondered how many of those people driving next to me, or perhaps walking nearby, might have also been worried about a family member's health or some other family crisis that may have been playing out for them. I wondered how many people around me were actually in the midst of what could be life or death experiences involving a loved one, or even themselves.

In those moments I found myself reflecting on how many people likely go through very serious and frequently life-changing experiences every single day. Many individuals are also actively helping others through a given experience. To some extent this might speak to a tendency among some people to take life itself for granted. But even more so I believe this dynamic speaks to how self-centered our society is… how so many people spend each day driving next to one another, walking by one another, and even working with people without truly "seeing" them. We spend so much of our lives in the presence of other people without giving a second thought to the "life" that is playing out just behind that thin veil we see.

It reinforced for me the clear sense of how precious life is. As an extension, it also reinforced for me a guiding life "ethic" if you will… always be "mindful" and "present" whenever you greet and interact with others – even strangers. You never know what others are dealing with as you see them on the street, pass by them on the highway, or even interact with them at work. Every smile and act of kindness can make a difference.

Now let me connect this to the point of this essay. There are some professions that, by their nature, seem to require a deeper sense of humanity and a deep appreciation for the seriousness – and complexity – of human life in all of its dimensions (e.g. physical, spiritual, mental, social, etc.). I thought about this in a more conscious way as my relative was in surgery. Doctors, surgeons in particular for the purpose of this analysis, have to be very *mindful* and *present* (in the deeper sense of these terms) because of the seriousness and delicate nature of their work. While I know my relative's surgery was more routine than some other types of surgery, I can't help but assume that even that surgeon remained keenly aware of how serious his role was.

I'm smart enough to know that surgeons are not all the same, but my vision of the serious nature of a surgeon's work is largely informed by my understanding of one exemplar's career in particular. I believe an examination of how this exemplar approaches his work has the potential to help us reflect critically on the way we think about our work in child welfare, and all professions that touch the lives of families for that matter.

An Exemplar in the Medical Healing Tradition

I'm not sure about all of you, but when I think about the work of a surgeon, especially the delicate nature of some surgeries, I typically think of Dr. Benjamin Carson. Dr. Carson is the world renowned African American neurosurgeon at Johns Hopkins University, and from none other than… you guessed it… Detroit, Michigan. He is widely recognized for his role in successfully performing numerous challenging surgeries, most notably the multiple successful surgical separations of twins attached at the head. I've read some of his writings and am very impressed with the sense of humility, dedication, and confidence he projects with respect to his work.

In his writing as well as in presentations I have heard him deliver, Dr. Carson speaks of how serious he takes his work on the one hand, but also his sense of clarity that he is a vessel through which the Creator and a universal healing energy are able to transform the lives of patients (read *The Big Picture;* as well as *Gifted Hands*). I remember Dr. Carson describing his routine in preparing for his most challenging surgeries. According to his description he spends his earliest time reading the medical charts of his patients so he can be as familiar as possible with what has already been documented about the patient's history and medical circumstances. As an extension of this process he also meets with the doctors and other medical personnel most familiar with the patient's medical history and circumstances.

Knowing that the written record only describes so much, he describes spending a great deal of time actually meeting with and getting to know the patients, the patients' family and those extended family members closest to the patients. In meeting with patients and their family members, he is particularly interested in verifying what he has read in the patients' charts on the one hand, but also learning what the charts most often do not describe… the patients' own perspectives on their health and present medical circumstances, any fears and/or anxiety related to the impending surgery, as well as their hopes, goals and plans for life post-surgery.

As much as he tries to gather information that will help him during his preparation and the actual surgery, he is also trying to counsel the patients and family members through the process. This includes helping the family members understand what is about to happen, the possible risks involved, and also helping to reassure them that he and the entire surgical team will take their time and do everything possible to ensure a successful outcome. If appropriate given the religious and spiritual beliefs of the patient and family members, he also joins them in prayer. After taking the time to get to know the family and gather as much information as possible, Dr. Carson meets with the entire surgical team (sometimes up to fifty or sixty people) and walks through every aspect of the surgery. He then spends the remainder of his time reflecting on the patient's case and visualizing the surgical procedure from start to finish – including all of the "what if scenarios" – with the most successful possible outcome in his mind.

In the operating room Dr. Carson and the surgical team have soothing classical and/or other inspirational music playing in the background for the duration of the surgery. They set up and arrange all of the medical equipment and supplies so that everything is easily accessible and most conducive to the technical requirements of the surgery, as well as comfortable for the patient and the surgical team. Many of these particularly complex surgeries can last upwards of twenty-four hours or more, taxing the physical and mental stamina of the entire surgical team. They frequently divide the surgical procedure into phases or stages, with all of the surgical team members present and prepared for any unexpected complications. When individuals involved on the surgical team are not actively participating in a particular stage of the operation, they are usually in a nearby room watching the procedure via closed circuit television. Communication is critical during these operations, as a successful outcome in this kind of effort depends on the ability of the entire team to work well together from start to finish.

What also strikes me about Dr. Carson's description is his insistence that much of his success during the most challenging surgeries is guided by a higher spiritual force. In many of his surgeries he can only see a limited section of the actual brain, nervous system and circulatory system as he is operating. In his description of the surgical separation of a set of twins from Zambia, Dr. Carson describes his sense of being a vessel through which the Creator could accomplish what "only He could do."

During this long and exhausting surgery, there was a particularly challenging part of the surgery that was put on hold until the end. Earlier during the surgery the team encountered an area with blood vessels so entangled that it looked like what Dr. Carson referred to as a "huge tangled serving of spaghetti." These veins were critical as they connected both of the boys' brains. As Dr. Carson continues to describe, this knot of blood vessels and the surrounding area were under so much pressure "they threatened a massive hemorrhage at the slightest mistake with even the tiniest of veins." Dr. Carson, among others on the surgical team, was exhausted by the time they completed all of the other critical stages of the surgery. By now, this final major task "looked even more imposing and hopeless than it had seemed when we had still been relatively fresh early that morning."

At the nineteen hour mark, Dr. Carson consulted with the surgical team about whether to continue with this last delicate stage of the surgery or postpone it until the team was able to recover and restore their energy. It was the unanimous opinion of the team that they should continue, fearful that if they didn't the boys might not make it through this period of partial separation. With that assessment, Dr. Carson realized they didn't have much of a choice. As he walked down the hall back to the operating room he concluded that "whatever will happen will happen." He prayed during that walk that God would take over the surgery and simply use him "to accomplish what only God could do." Dr. Carson reflects: "Despite the exhaustion that had almost paralyzed me a short time earlier, I now sensed an incredible steadiness in my hands. I felt a strange calm, an almost detached awareness - as if I were merely watching my hands move and someone else had actually taken over the surgery." (p.40, *The Big picture*)

By the end of the surgery the boys were already showing signs of neurological functioning. Despite the huge challenges and sheer exhaustion, the surgery was a tremendous success. Dr. Carson recounted that it was very common for him to talk to and reflect with the parents and family members of the children after the operations, and that the families frequently share with him how they continued to pray throughout the procedure for a successful outcome. He also shares with them his own experience praying before, as well as throughout, the procedure.

My intent here is not to focus on religion and spirituality, but to highlight the level of focus, concentration, and mindfulness as he approaches his work. This intense concentration is present from the earliest stages of involvement with a patient through the post-surgical and recovery period. He is very much interested and invested in achieving successful outcomes for each and every one of his patients.

Healing and the Human Services

In a general sense, one could argue that the work of individuals involved in the human services is not all that different than the nature of the contribution of these surgeons and their surgical teams. Certainly the tools of our trade are very different, but the substance of our work is intended to serve a similar purpose… we seek to support children, families and communities in ways that improve their ability to live healthy and productive lives.

Let's take a closer look at the work of child welfare systems. The mission statement of many child welfare systems usually includes a reference to promoting the well-being of families, as well as ensuring that all children have the opportunity to grow up in safe and "permanent" families.

While we don't frequently talk about our work in such terms, so much of our work is really about supporting the "healing" and development of families and family systems, especially when a family's challenges are perceived to pose a threat to the well-being of children. In this context, healing does not presuppose that families are *sick* or otherwise *broken.* Rather, "healing" refers to the process of supporting families in an attempt to make families healthier and stronger, and thus improving their capacity to care for their children. Our work can rightly be viewed as healing work.

Let me be clearer here. That's what our work *could* and *should* be about. Unfortunately, however, this is not typically the lens through which child welfare practice is viewed or performed. Too often the work of child welfare systems has become the legally mandated intervention by bureaucratic systems in an effort to "save" children from real or potential maltreatment. As a natural outgrowth of this mission, child welfare systems are frequently charged with identifying children in potentially harmful situations, removing them from such situations, and placing them in what are assumed to be more safe and stable living environments. The child welfare system then assumes the responsibility of gathering evidence to justify its intervention, and developing criteria that must be met in order for a child to be reunified with her or his family of origin. Child welfare officials typically refer families to any support services and resources they know are available and believe may be effective given what they know about a particular family and their "needs." As much as this approach might be guided by "good intentions," this is not the same as what I envision as "healing" work.

A Healing Vision for Child Welfare

Can you imagine what a child welfare system could be like if we actually approached it with the same care, dedication and humility described by Dr. Ben Carson? What would child welfare look like if direct service child welfare professionals actually saw and approached their roles as that of *healing agents* and not as "case-carrying" and "case-managing" social workers? What if people in my line of work (improving systems) saw our role as helping to prepare and support human service professionals to be more effective in their critically important role as healing agents?

<u>A Prepared Workforce</u>

Imagine a workforce that was expected to be intimately familiar with the historical underpinnings of a given community's present day social, spiritual, political, and economic dynamics. Imagine a workforce that was familiar with this history as it related to both the formal institutional makeup of the community, as well as the racial and ethnic composition of the community. Imagine a workforce that was also intimately familiar with the historical context of the various human service systems, and the nature of their interaction with various geographic as well as racial / ethnic communities. By human service systems I am referring to the public *and* private sectors of these various systems. Imagine a workforce that was familiar with and understood the interconnectedness of all of these dynamics, and was able to view a family's challenges – including the historical and multi-generational antecedents of these challenges – in this broader context.

Furthermore, imagine a public child welfare agency whose doors are open to the community-at-large. Such an agency would welcome and actively seek out the participation of community members, civic leaders, youth and families with prior child welfare system involvement, members of the faith community and representatives from community based organizations in the agency's ongoing system improvement, policy reform and continuous quality improvement efforts. In doing so, agencies would be assured of moving forward in ways that are consistent with a community's vision for optimal child and family well-being.

Of course the above community engagement approach would assume that communities are organized and actively engaged in executing an agenda for the continued growth and development of healthy families and children. If the broader community is not organized in such a way, the public child welfare agency can proactively develop community partnerships and coalitions that would in turn begin to develop this neighborhood and community safety net and well-being agenda. Such deliberate efforts should be very mindful of engaging the indigenous community organizers, community leaders and community based organizations, assuming that they are most familiar with the historical and present day trends and dynamics in a given community.

Minimum Intrusion & Family Connections

Imagine a child welfare profession that uniformly respected the principle of minimum intrusion. Such a field would seek to intervene in a family's affairs only when it was clearly demonstrated that children were at risk of being maltreated. Even in such cases, child welfare professionals would do everything possible to support these families while leaving the children at home with their families. The first line of response to these families would naturally be the indigenous and other community organizations that make up the neighborhood safety net. Children would only be removed from their parents when it could be demonstrated that they had been or were truly at imminent risk of being harmed. Even in these extreme circumstances social workers would do everything possible to place these children with extended family members as opposed to strangers (except of course under those extreme circumstances where this would jeopardize their safety).

Even in extreme circumstances, when a child must be removed from her/his parents, a healing-oriented organization and professional would recognize its responsibility to engage families as long as necessary to help them through the traumatic experience of having a child removed. In some cases this means beginning a genuine effort to support reunification; in other cases it might mean counseling families through the legal process of having their parental rights terminated.

I would argue, however, that a profession truly committed to healing and honoring natural family relationships would abandon the standard child welfare approach (and I would argue archaic notion) of "termination of parental rights." There are other ways to recognize changes in "legal" parenting relationships and responsibilities without deliberately disconnecting a child from her or his natural parents and extended family members. In this case the nation's legal system would also have to recognize its role in supporting individual and family healing dynamics. I feel strongly about this because it's not only the child-parent relationship that is affected by the removal of children from their homes of origin. Other individuals affected by these decisions include the child's relatives and the family's extended family support network, not to mention any additional friends of the young child. You can think of these, as author and poet Jaiya John articulates, as "rippling effects" that touch people in varying ways depending on their closeness to the child and immediate family members.

Initial Contact

Now let's imagine what an agency's initial contact with a family might look like. Imagine the group of professionals responsible for the child welfare agency's initial contact with families being genuinely considered family resource professionals and not "child protective services" workers. That title itself is very presumptive and speaks volumes to a family about the agency's assumptions about them upon initial contact.

After receiving a report that a family might be struggling, imagine these family resource workers being able to take the time needed to truly understand the dynamics playing out with a given family… talking with the numerous individuals that could best inform them of a family's assets and strengths, challenges (including the full historical context and contributing factors) and desires for their own future. Imagine the social workers having the time, as well as the engagement skills, necessary to really begin to develop and nurture a meaningful and trusting relationship with a family.

Working as a Team In Support of Families

When further engagement with a family is necessary, imagine a collective of professionals and other individuals close to a given family forming a well-functioning team that provides the assistance, support, encouragement and guidance a family needs. This team would include specialists that have the resources needed to respond effectively to the educational needs of a child *and family members*, the substance abuse treatment and/or other mental health needs of a child *and family members*, any basic material needs of a child *and family members* (including housing), any child care and supervision needs of the family, as well as any of the other needs identified by the team of professionals and family members. This would ideally be a team guided by the family (includes extended family) and supported by the professionals connected with the various human service systems. Their approach would be holistic.

This team would not only meet during the case planning process and/or to make critical decisions regarding the family and children's future. Each member of the team would also be responsible for supporting the family and children in very clearly defined roles, all helping to ensure a successful outcome for the children and the larger family. More significantly, the entire family and extended family support network would play a critical role in informing the larger team of a family's strengths, challenges, available natural supports and resources, as well as aspirations. Through this kind of process human service professionals are able to take the necessary time to actually "see" and engage more effectively with the families they are working with.

Work Environment

Imagine the physical facilities designed to support the work of the various human services. Imagine families being able to meet with social workers and other human service professionals in settings that are warm and inviting for children and families. This would include the setup of the office, the furniture, the lighting and color schemes as well as special attention given to the space where families are initially greeted. Imagine professional settings with artwork and other forms of cultural expression that celebrate the diverse background of its workforce as well as the families that are served by a given office. Imagine images of children and families decorating the walls of the human service buildings, a reminder to the workforce of why they do their work. Imagine signs and other inspirational quotes and words of encouragement for both staff as well as families. The physical dimensions of the workplace should acknowledge, celebrate and affirm the humanity and value of the families and the professionals doing the work.

Imagine social workers having office space that facilitates thoughtful and reflective practice, as well as access to space for relaxing, unwinding and decompressing after handling some of the more stressful dynamics presented by some families and children. Imagine social workers having access to state of the art technology that facilitates information sharing about families as well as about the various community support services and resources available to assist families.

Social Worker Training / Professional Development

Imagine a standard social work training process that – as the norm – familiarizes aspiring social workers with the indigenous spiritual and healing traditions of the communities in which they are serving (and others around the world for that matter), and helps social workers understand how to tap into these various traditions in ways that enhance their ability to work with diverse groups of children and families. Imagine a social work field that normalizes the expectation that some social workers will be more or less effective in engaging some children, families and circumstances. Within such a workforce operational framework supervisors will have the ability and flexibility to match workers up with families based on what they know of the workers' strengths and the particularities of a given family's strengths, challenges and/or other dynamics.

Advocacy & Cross-Systems Leadership

In such a system the roles of social workers and social worker supervisors would not just be to make sure the agency's legal interests are protected, or even to ensure minimal or "reasonable efforts" are made to match families up with the resources available to support them. Social workers, their supervisors, as well as senior level child welfare administrators that acknowledge a "healing function" of their role would advocate relentlessly on behalf of the families they are working with. They would be unrelenting advocates for the support services, financial resources, or other forms of support and services they know would be beneficial to the families they work with. It would be unacceptable to such workers and administrators to see families struggle and be torn apart largely because of the lack of available support services and resources that would otherwise help to resolve some of the major challenges facing individuals and families.

In many instances this new advocacy role on behalf of families will require child welfare professionals and leaders to actively engage professionals and leaders in other human service and related systems (e.g. substance abuse, mental health, housing, public assistance, education, etc.) to make the resources available that families genuinely need in order to be healthier and well. When resources that have been shown to be necessary are not made available (and in a timely manner), child welfare agency leaders must actively engage executive level government officials to make these resources available. Through its community partnerships, these same child welfare officials can help to generate and apply additional external pressure on public officials to make resources available for families.

Policy and Legal Implications

Judges and legal representatives would play an increasingly important role in ensuring that families receive the supports and resources that would be most helpful, and within timeframes that are most appropriate. Also with respect to timelines, judges would exercise the flexibility allowed to assist families in completing substance abuse treatment programs and/or other efforts that are designed to support their healing and develop their capacity to care for their children.

Policy makers must also realize their role in supporting the continued healing and development of families and children. They have direct responsibility for making and/or amending specific laws and regulations that guide the allocation of support services and other resources that currently are or would be helpful to families. They also have the ability to guide child welfare agencies in their execution of practices and strategies that have proven effective in healing families and producing optimal outcomes for children and families. Examples of such strategies and practices might include the identification and engagement of fathers and paternal relatives; effective engagement of families in the case planning and decision making process; use of data to track outcomes for families and children; developing performance improvement requirements for organizations working with children and families of specific racial / ethnic groups; among others.

A Sense of Urgency and Purpose

What if we all committed ourselves to not only doing our jobs well (although in most cases that's probably a good thing), but also to transforming the way people think about and respond to struggling families and their children. Moreover, what if we all started today, with the next person we interact with; be it a family involved with the child welfare system, a coworker or even a neighbor. Everyone has a role to play and every day is critical for our children waiting in foster care.

Among the Akan people of Ghana in West Africa, there is an Adinkra symbol that speaks to the potential for human change and transformation. *Sesa Wo Suban* literally means "Change or transform my character," and is frequently used to refer to life transformation. One of our goals, if approaching this work through a healing lens, is to help create the conditions in which healing and self/family-transformation is most likely to occur. But our assumption is that given the right circumstances and the appropriate amount of time, all parents, families and children can.

This is Doable!

In presenting the above ideas and possibilities I am not assuming that some of these practices, strategies, and organizational management efforts don't exist in part or even in totality in some places. Even in the time that I have been working in child welfare I have seen some unique and innovative approaches to child welfare practice. What I am arguing for is an approach to child welfare and human services in this country where these things are no longer seen as unique and innovative, but rather the norm and the standard by which we measure effective child welfare system functioning.

I would argue that in order to get there as a field, we have to appreciate our role, not as bureaucratic servants or child saving professionals, but as *healing agents* in service of families and communities. We have to recognize that our work in many ways is just as influential as that of other professions in either supporting or harming the likelihood of families becoming healthier and stronger.

We are certainly not there yet as a field, but we can definitely get there. And we can do so in our lifetime!

Fourteen

Why I Write What I Like...
And Why You Should Too!

September 12, 2010
(Previously Unpublished)

"I write what I like because I have observations, experiences and perspectives to share that I think are critically important, yet missing from many important conversations about the needs and interests of African American children, families and communities. I think you should do the same because your observations, experiences and perspectives are equally as important."

One of the consistent questions people have asked me over the last couple of years is, "What made you start writing these essays?" My response is usually brief, but the reality of why I initially started writing these essays deserves a bit more attention – especially since deciding to publish the essays and share with a wider audience. This fuller explanation, I believe, is also critical in appreciating why these essays should be read by not only those who work with or on behalf of children and families, but by everyone interested in the healing and development of African American families and communities.

Most directly, I started writing these essays because of how I was introduced to the professional world of child welfare, and how all of my subsequent professional experiences have been so tremendously different – indeed even alarming at times. More indirectly, however, I started writing these essays because of my cumulative experiences (growing up in Detroit, during my college years at Howard University, as well as during my early professional years in child welfare) trying to make sense of why so many people with tremendously important stories to share and ideas to offer were frequently missing from – in the professional and societal-public realms – the critical conversations about how to improve the life experiences of African American children and families. The essays in this book, indeed the book itself, are my attempts to help "advance the conversation" and create a larger and more integrity-centered space in which these conversations are able to happen.

While at some point I'd like to explore the fuller experiences referenced in the previous paragraph, my focus in this essay will be the theme "why I write what I like." The reason I write what I like is because I have a perspective to share that I believe is critically important, yet either completely missing from or under-explored within the larger conversations about African American families and children, especially those caught up in the storm of this nation's child welfare and juvenile justice systems. The more personal side of this, however, is my own many experiences that have instilled within me a commitment to speaking truth and passion in settings where it is sadly missing yet critically needed, and in settings where I believe it is being deliberately silenced or marginalized. Some of those are the experiences and reflections I'll share in this essay.

Social and Political Education Begins at Home

Growing up in Detroit during the 1970's and 80's, it was quite easy for me to recognize the pervasive nature of White racism and oppression, as well as the resulting pathology among a good number of people and communities on the receiving end of it. This pathology was evident in the violence and crime that plagued predominantly African American inner city Detroit. When you compared the experiences of the City of Detroit and its predominantly African American residents to the experiences of the then-blossoming and predominantly White suburbs, the impacts of racism were easily visible in the day-to-day life experiences of people, and within the fabric of metropolitan Detroit's institutions and societal dynamics.

While I didn't fully understand how the dynamics of structural and institutional racism worked at the time, there were some implications that were obvious. Increasingly during my childhood years there was a huge focus, in the media and in institutional settings, on the "vanishing Black male," "the violent Black male predator," and Black men as an "endangered species." There were an increasing number of conferences, emergency town hall meetings, community forums, and other initiatives devoted to figuring out the root causes of the Black-on-Black violence that claimed the lives of so many Black men and boys. Detroit was becoming widely known as the murder capitol of the world. The issue of the day was the escalating crisis facing Black males.

While the dynamic was indeed real, part of this experience growing up was strange to me because so many of the youth I grew up with, and went to high school with, weren't as directly caught up in the madness, and were, for the most part, staying out of trouble and doing the right things. Indeed, it was hard not to be directly affected by the crime and violence, as most families were touched by it in one way or another. But the point here is that most of the youth I knew were still doing the right things, and didn't fit the bill in terms of the images and messages being sold to us in the popular media. During these later years in high school I became fixated on trying to understand why African Americans were seemingly so despised and thus disparaged by the media and other societal institutions, yet we fully embodied (at times to a fault) the so-called American ideals of achievement, hard-work, pursuit of higher education, and an unwavering faith in God.

For a long time, I kept my struggles with these ideas and contradictions to myself. In search of an explanation, I began to browse the volumes of books on African American history and culture my parents had on our basement bookshelves. During my senior year in high school, however, I began having explicit conversations about some of these dynamics with my father. Those were some of the first conversations I remember having about racism, politics, and the experiences of African people in this country over the last several hundred years. The contradictions I was beginning to learn more about were further highlighted by the many positive and influential experiences I had while participating in leadership development programs at our church and those sponsored by Kappa Alpha Psi Fraternity, Inc., particularly the members of the Detroit Alumni Chapter.

Increasingly, I began to visit the Shrine of the Black Madonna Bookstore and Cultural Center during my free time and on weekends, to explore more books about African people and our experiences in this country and around the world. One of the first books I bought with my own money was *Countering the Conspiracy to Destroy Black Boys* by Jawanza Kunjufu. The ideas in this very small book helped to shape my early understandings of how the complex and internalized dynamics of racism in American society work to create profoundly negative outcomes for African American children, reinforced by the ideas and actions of both institutions and individuals. Months after buying that book someone told me about a book by Anthony Browder entitled *From the Browder File*, a collection of essays exploring the history of African people and the ways in which White racism and cultural oppression have shaped the experiences of African people in this country. Even during these early years, this book was critical in shaping my appreciation of how each of us has the ability, responsibility, and the creative capacity to share the truth about our people and our experiences in this society.

High School Experiences

While all of these critically important influences and experiences were shaping my early ideas about race, place and space in this country, I was very aware that they were all coming from individuals and settings outside of school. Increasingly, I was becoming frustrated by the lack of access to information and discussions within the formal school setting that were explicitly about and related to the experiences of African people in this country.

During all of my high school years, I don't recall any courses with dedicated time devoted to the African American experience, except for the annual obligatory rush to cover all of "Black" History during the designated February timeframe. Moreover, I can only remember two high school teachers that expressed frustration with this crazy dynamic. One of the teachers was an African American social studies teacher that complained to students about the narrow content focus of the school's selected course materials (I believe during my freshman or sophomore year). The other teacher was ironically a White mathematics teacher who periodically integrated within his lessons various historical references intended to serve as a reminder to students that much of what the world knows about mathematics comes from our African ancestors. His intent clearly was to inspire students to better understand our fundamental relationship to the information we were being taught.

The two individuals mentioned above were the exceptions by far. Most of my teachers were not so progressively inclined. To this day, I am clear that one of my most influential high school teachers was my Advanced Placement (AP) English teacher. It was the series of experiences I had with this African American teacher that increased my passion and commitment to help tell a different story about the experiences of African people in this country. As a part of the AP English class, we spent a great deal of time reading the European literary classics, as well as writing essays and speeches about various topics. In terms of the technical training the teacher was charged with providing students, she was exceptional. I clashed with her repeatedly, however, because of what I experienced as her consistent and explicit refusal to allow me to express my ideas and opinions about the material and topics being discussed in class.

During my high school years, it was routine for corporations, businesses and other organizations within the community to sponsor writing contests and oratorical / speech contests to showcase the "talented and gifted" students in the metropolitan Detroit area. Ironically, many of the topics for the essay and speech contests had themes related to aspirations and goals for students, civic / community engagement and participation, reflections on how far society had come with respect to Black history, and other related themes. I always wrote essays and developed speeches that reflected my honest opinions and assessments. I frequently pointed out the contradictions (as I saw them) in the topics we were asked to write about, the insidious racism that I continued to see in the metropolitan Detroit area, and what seemed to me to be continuing injustices faced by Black folks in America. While the teacher was complimentary of the technical aspects of the essays and speeches I wrote and developed, she refused to submit my writings and speeches for consideration in the various competitions. I recall her continuously making comments about how the pieces were well written and developed, but absolutely inappropriate because of the content. I recall her becoming increasingly frustrated with my insistence on developing my essays and speeches with these consistent themes.

This back and forth dynamic and tension worsened during the months leading up to graduation at the end of senior year. I was the president of my senior class in high school, and as such, was expected to make comments at the graduation ceremony. As the lead teacher within the English department, this same AP English teacher had the responsibility of coordinating with all of the students that were to have speaking roles at graduation, and make sure we received any assistance we needed in preparing. This "assistance in preparing" included an expectation that she review all of our speeches and practice them with us in advance of graduation day. Given all of the things I was beginning to read outside of school, the contradictions I was becoming more aware of regarding race and the experience of African American people, the increasing demonization of young Black males in society, as well as the experience I was having with this teacher throughout my senior year, I had no interest in whatever feedback she might have or assistance she might provide. I was clear by then that my graduation speech should include comments about the inexcusable absence of any critical discussion or coverage of African history and culture in the school curriculum.

I avoided talking with the English teacher about my speech for weeks leading up to graduation. I had been preparing the speech, but I was absolutely insistent that she shouldn't be in a position of censoring my remarks. Graduation day came, and we finally saw each other in the room where all of the administrators, dignitaries from the school board and other students who were to be on stage were gathering. She commented that we had been missing each other and that she hadn't had an opportunity to review my speech before hand. She asked if she could still review it, and I complied. After reviewing it, she shook her head and confirmed what I always suspected her reaction would be. She immediately lectured me (in her professional way) about how my speech was accusatory, and that it was inappropriate to offer such critical reflections during what was supposed to be a celebratory occasion. She went on to point out the several members of the school board and the representatives of the superintendent's office for the Detroit Public Schools who were present, and how this was not the appropriate occasion for expressing my personal opinions. She told me that she knew I had strong feelings and ideas, but that she sincerely hoped I would reconsider my decision to share those remarks between that moment and when I stood up at the podium.

Not a chance. I was even more incensed! I began my remarks by talking about the exciting and celebratory nature of the occasion for all of my wonderful classmates and our families, all of the important lessons and great moments we experienced during our high school years, and the many memories we would take with us as we entered the next stages of each of our respective journeys. I then looked directly at my English teacher and began my final reflections. In those final few minutes, I reflected on the inexcusable contradiction, as I saw it, for such a large school system that is predominantly African American, and run by predominantly African American men and women, to not have any required courses about the history of African people in this country or abroad, and not have any literature by or about African American authors as a part of the required readings in any of our English or literature classes. After the graduation ceremony, I saw my teacher again in the same room after we marched out of the large gymnasium and – true to form – she complimented me on a thoughtful and well developed speech, but reiterated that she still thought it was the wrong message at the wrong time and in the wrong place. She then complimented me on my courage and persistence, and wished me the best of luck in the future.

I've never seen or heard from that teacher since that day, but she remains one of the most influential teachers I've had in all of my years of formal education. My experience with her significantly shaped my early strong feelings about: 1) the critical importance of creating spaces where African American people can talk about the issues that are important to us without being filtered through a lens of those who might either be offended, threatened by, or otherwise uncomfortable with our perspectives; and 2) the critical importance of affirming the legitimacy of everyone's perspective when based on their own experience and reflective analysis.

The Michigan Chronicle

Inspired by my frustration and even resentment about the dynamics culminating around the end of my senior year, I was intent on finding some sort of public outlet to share my frustration and raise my voice. Through my mom and dad, I had long been familiar with the Michigan Chronicle (Detroit's historic African American newspaper) and was always excited about reading the critical perspectives and some level of truth-telling that could be found in the paper. I decided to write a very long essay that I was hoping would be included on the paper's Commentary page. Much of that essay was about my perceptions and analysis of a racist and hypocritical media, the unjust treatment and targeting of African American politicians (primarily Coleman A. Young and Marion Barry in that essay), and the biased coverage of the challenges confronting the African American community in general, and those confronting African American youth in particular.

I bought and searched a copy of the paper every week for the rest of that summer, and even tried to follow up with the editor by phone a couple of times, but the essay was never printed. Admittedly, the essay was very long and rambling, but it was one of my first attempts at sharing publically a perspective that I thought was clearly missing and intentionally marginalized. Indeed, this was a passion and an ethic that really began to form for me in high school, and continued to form – and be challenged – well into my undergraduate and graduate school years.

Undergraduate College Experiences

There were a number of occasions at Howard University – especially experiences in the School of Education – that were frustrating and discouraging in ways similar to the high school experiences described above. The first experience I'll share was with a professor in a course on the social underpinnings of urban educational practice. This course featured readings and texts that included theories about the racial achievement gap in many urban school systems. It was in this class that we were introduced to the writings and/or ideas of Asa G. Hilliard, A. Wade Boykin, Gloria Ladson Billings, Carol Lee, John Ogbu, Roslyn A. Mickelson, Signithia Fordham, Thomas Sowell, among others.

While I count this class among the most enjoyable courses I took during my undergraduate years at Howard, it was my interaction with the professor that simultaneously made it one of the most frustrating and disappointing. The professor in this particular class was an African gentleman, originally from central Africa. He frequently created space for critical dialogue and debate in his class, which I loved. What was discouraging, however, was his continuous insistence that my (and several other students') passion and fervor for African-centered ideas and ideals was but a passing phase that would quickly disappear as we had more experience in the "real world." He equated it with the passion and zeal of many of his contemporaries during the 1960's civil rights era and the so-called radicalism of the free-love Woodstock era and generation. While the intellectual and anti-war activism and idealism among many in that generation peaked during their college years, many of the individuals became measurably more conservative and mainstream in their opinions and perspectives as they became institutionalized (professionally and occupationally speaking) during their post-college years.

At face value one might not find a problem with the professor's position. Indeed his observations may appear to make sense, especially given his experience. The problem, though, is that he increasingly seemed to lightheartedly dismiss many of the analyses and arguments that some of us offered about the schooling dynamics and challenges we were observing as being clouded by our youthful radicalism and inexperience. Once we entered the "real world" of urban education, he continued to argue, we would appreciate that the real challenges were related to a deepening pathology within African American families and communities (lack of value for education, lack of parent involvement, lack of parent expectations and goals for children, etc.). I felt strongly at that time (and still do now) that this explanation is very superficial, and reflects little to no appreciation and analysis of the complexity of the racial and cultural experience of people of African ancestry in this country. Moreover, I thought the substance and the tone of the professor's persistent comments gave some of the students a pass, if you will, and failed to challenge many of our classmates to articulate a more critical analysis of what we were observing in urban educational trends and teaching practices.

Another college experience I'll share is a multi-faceted experience I had with one of the deans of the Howard University School of Education. This particular experience came about after one dean resigned, and the new dean was beginning her tenure. The outgoing dean was by all accounts African-centered and progressive in her views and theories of education. She clearly articulated her perspective regarding the ways in which the history of racism and cultural oppression in the United States has contributed to the pattern of failure we witness in the attempts of large urban school systems to meet the educational needs of large numbers of African American children and communities. Also noteworthy was the outgoing dean's proactive encouragement of and support for student activism, particularly in our efforts to raise awareness of and build solutions for satisfying the unmet needs of African American and other under-achieving communities involved with this nation's school systems. The incoming dean was notably more conservative in her appreciation for – or even basic tolerance of – student activism and involvement in leading discussions about the needed reforms within this nation's school systems.

I was among a group of students involved with the School of Education student council during that school year. Our primary goal was to increase student participation in discussions about the potential causes of and solutions for the chronic underachievement of African American children in this nation's school systems. We wanted to partner with the incoming school administration in leading these discussions. Those summer months preceding the school year and the first couple of months of the school year were tense.

During the summer months, and as president of the School of Education student council, I presented to the incoming dean the student council's plans for the upcoming school year, largely organized around a year-long lecture series the student council would sponsor and organize. The featured speakers were to include such noted educational and history scholars as Asa G. Hilliard, Barbara Sizemore, Russell Adams, Anthony Browder, as well as a number of individuals involved with the local public school system's ongoing fight over African-centered education. The incoming dean's initial reaction seemed particularly personal and harsh. She confronted me in the narrow hallway of the School of Education building, just outside of her office. I was accused of being narrow minded, not thinking for myself, allowing myself to be manipulated by the outgoing dean, and she said she wouldn't support the lecture series the student council was organizing. The tone for the upcoming school year was marked by a great deal of tension (even hostility at the beginning) and a strong distrust between the incoming administration and the increasingly active and assertive student council.

Members of the student council were increasingly frustrated with the early tone of the relationship between the student council and the incoming administration, and our overall frustration with what we saw as the alarming silence among faculty members and many students within the School of Education about the dismal experiences of too many African American children in this nation's school systems. As was customary with the start of each new school year, the student council president was invited to participate in the School of Education's annual back-to-school program to welcome everyone back for a new year, especially helpful for new students and faculty. The occasion was even more important for the school given the change in administrations during the preceding summer.

I was excited about the opportunity to share the student council's vision, plan and commitment to fostering increased dialogue about the experiences and needs of African American children in this nation's school systems. I also wanted to do something dramatic and creative in order to catch people's attention and reinforce our message. After talking through the idea with a few other student council leaders, I decided to structure my presentation as that of a judge presiding over a court, and rendering the verdict on a contentious case. My comments were fairly straight forward.

I opened my presentation by stating that the students were charging the Howard University School of Education with failing to prepare teachers who could effectively teach

African American children. As such, and secondly, the students were charging the Howard University School of Education with ultimately contributing to the mis-education of African American children by failing to advocate effectively for needed reforms. The evidence presented on behalf of the students was the dismal educational statistics in terms of the racial achievement gap, and the generally poor outcomes for African American children with respect to relative rates of subject matter mastery, high school completion, and subsequent college enrollment and completion.

I then moved on to the verdict... After reflecting on our experiences – and the response of the School of Education faculty and administrators to our concerns – the student council had met (as the jury representing our peers) and was prepared to offer the final verdict / opinion. In our reflection and conclusion we found the Howard University School of Education guilty of mis-educating African American children, specifically because of… a) its failure to produce teachers who could reflect critically on the experiences of African American children and families involved with this nation's school systems, and b) its failure to produce solutions for the widespread under-achievement of African American children involved with this nation's school systems.

After my presentation, there was an uncomfortable silence in the auditorium. To say the presentation was not warmly received would be a great understatement. The dean – who was visibly angry in the moment – made a few polite yet critical remarks about my presentation, and quickly moved on with the program. In the days and weeks following the program, I was called to the dean's office, the associate dean's office, my academic advisor's office, and was likewise invited to meet with many of the department chairs within the School of Education. While the subsequent several meetings with the dean were emotionally charged and tense, my sense is that she was becoming increasingly more clear that the student council was serious about our goals for the year, and was intent on creating our own opportunities for dialogue that we were not getting in our courses. This was reinforced by our use of the Howard University student newspaper, *The Hilltop*, to share our ideas and advocate for more student involvement.

Over time, even though we seemed to disagree on our respective analyses – the dean and the student council developed a much more cooperative working relationship. Additionally, while the associate dean was clear in saying he thought the tactic used at the back-to-school event was a little unfair to the professors and administrators, he supported the underlying intent and our commitment to creating a space for critical discussion and debate – all based on critical analysis and reflection. Virtually all of the other professors and department chairs expressed similar sentiments. Over time, some of these individuals would become great supporters of our efforts, and advocates for our activities, as the year progressed. More importantly, they would become increasingly instrumental in helping students reflect more critically on the creation of improved educational outcomes for specific groups of underachieving children, especially within African American and other under-achieving communities.

For some context, one should keep in mind here that – especially on college campuses – many students frequently see themselves as the primary customer of a service that the university is being paid to provide. As such, it makes perfect sense that students – as the customers – have a right to offer feedback on whether the product they are receiving is of the quality and standard they desire and expect. I am clear now that the dynamics are a little more complicated than that, but I still believe the basic idea is legitimate. I also believe this idea about education must extend beyond just the higher education setting. The entire educational endeavor, at its core, should be driven by a critical dialogue and engagement between the designated instructors (who are presumed to have some skill and ability to support a student's development) and the students (who must enter into the process with a willingness to engage and learn). Education (and professional development I might add) in its truest form has to be a process of critical reflection and engagement between all of the participants in the process.

The bottom line for the student council at that time was that the curriculum (both substance and context) didn't embody this notion of education as a culturally-centered critical discourse, and thus the frustration of many students.

Moreover, the new administration was perceived as stifling – with a heavy hand at that – opportunities for critical reflection and discourse about the root causes for the educational challenges faced by many African American children. I experienced these instances as yet additional cases of individuals and institutions explicitly attempting to censor and/or marginalize my and other students' ideas and perspectives, and at times completely shut down opportunities for us to share our ideas and perspectives, our passion, and our yearning to make sense of the experiences of African American children, families and communities within this nation's educational systems and institutions.

What Information is Worthy of Consideration?

An additional and related dynamic that stood out to me during my undergraduate years, which continued during my graduate school years, was the way in which professors actually incorporated materials written by or about African American people into the curriculum. At the beginning of every school year the instructor or professor handed out the course syllabus or outline that typically included a list of readings to be covered during the course. The course outline or syllabus typically included a list of "required readings" and sometimes an additional list of "supplemental readings." The required readings were seen as containing the leading ideas, theories, and practices from the field, were almost always written and produced by White individuals, and were developed and filtered through the lens of their personal and professional experiences (which are erroneously and arrogantly assumed to be universal). The materials written by leading African American professionals, theorists and practitioners were almost always included on the supplemental reading lists, if they were included or referenced at all. This was also true of reading materials specifically about the experiences of African American children, adults, families and communities – regardless of whether they were written by African American or other authors.

What I began to recognize during my later years in college and in graduate school was that the ways in which these course materials were being developed and presented didn't only shape *the kinds of information people were exposed to* in their professional studies and training programs. A larger impact was the way in which these schooling / training experiences, over time, shaped people's *perceptions of the relative value* of various sources of information and ideas.

A consistent observation of mine during college and graduate school, and a continuing observation of mine during my professional years, is that the ideas and contributions of African American authors and professionals were and continue to be seen by many as being parochial, or narrow in scope and relevance. As such, the ideas and contributions (previous and potential) of these very authors and professionals are discounted and marginalized. Access to opportunities for these individuals to participate in discussions among the influential and decision making professionals and administrators in various fields frequently depends on the extent to which their contributions - in substance and in tone - disrupt the zones of comfort in which these decision-makers and administrators currently operate and/or practice. I offer this observation based on my professional experience and my observation of others' professional experiences.

Concluding Thoughts

I have become clearer over the years that very little about the production and presentation of knowledge in this country is racially or culturally neutral. Yet, however, the perspectives and ideas of White professionals and scholars are somehow seen as being universal in their relevance and application, while those of African American professionals and scholars are seen as being narrowly relevant to the interests and experiences of African American people. This is a great loss to this nation's professions and fields of practice. Moreover, this unfounded arrogance and sense of superiority among too many White professionals and scholars prevents this country from benefitting from a huge reservoir of experience and expertise as it struggles to sustain itself at the dawn of a new century.

Throughout my high school, undergraduate, and subsequent graduate school years, as well as in my years in the professional world, I've had numerous experiences similar to those described above that have taught me a great deal about courage, integrity and the importance of speaking one's truth. I've learned that there is indeed a price to pay for speaking up and speaking out… and not remaining silent. Surely, it can cost you personal, educational and career-related networking opportunities, job opportunities, or perhaps even invitations to this or that special event. There are many people who tend not to want to spend time with or be associated with individuals who are considered "too serious," "trouble-makers," or who are seen as too likely to "rock the boat." Indeed, being outspoken can even cost you your job, your livelihood or even worse in extreme circumstances.

When it's all said and done, however, I'm growing to appreciate that the benefits generally tend to outweigh any of these losses – particularly when your truth is rooted in a firm commitment to an idea for which you are willing to work tirelessly. Despite the losses, what you gain is access to more personally meaningful opportunities that are more closely aligned with the real work you have committed yourself to doing. People also take you more seriously and don't tend to waste as much of your time. People approach you in noticeably more straightforward ways and about more serious issues, opportunities, events and activities. Certainly, the path forward still isn't always clear, and you will continue to run into various life challenges, but when you stay true to your values, your ideals, your calling and your inner voice, things will generally work out in your favor.

One of the challenges we face in this society is that there are many people, institutions and other mechanisms that actively distract us from even recognizing and acknowledging our own truth, our own ideas and perspectives, our own voice. Many students sit in classes and listen to lots of theories and explanations about things that seem completely off-base, or simply irrelevant to the kinds of challenges and dynamics we see in our communities. Many professionals sit in meetings, sit through trainings and participate in conversations about issues and potential solutions that we know don't get to the root causes of the kinds of challenges we are attempting to address. Yet many students and professionals too frequently remain silent and largely disengaged.

It is critically important that each one of us make the most of the time we have, and maximize the potential within the specific opportunities and moments presented to us. This means that each one of us has the responsibility of speaking our truth whenever we open our mouths. We must take those courageous next steps, advocate for and create the opportunities and resources we know are needed to meet the needs of African American children and families. I have always believed, and continue to believe, that the collective African American community has most (if not all) of the resources we need to meet the needs of our children, our families and our communities. Where we don't already have the resources, we certainly have the creative capacity to bring those resources into existence. It is up to us to heal and develop our children, families and communities.

The dynamics I attempt to describe and discuss in this essay are my reflections on individuals in positions of power and influence deciding what perspectives are appropriate or most worthy of being shared and discussed, and as a result which perspectives and ideas are inappropriate or less worthy to be shared and discussed. I write what I like because I have observations, experiences and perspectives to share that I think are critically important, yet missing from many important conversations about the needs and interests of African American children, families and communities. I think you should do the same because your observations, experiences and perspectives are equally as important. My challenge to you right now is to raise your own voice, tell your own story, and support others around you in doing the same!

FACT SHEET:

African American Children in America's Child Welfare System, Fiscal Year 2006

General Child Population

- There were approximately 73.5 million children in the United States population in 2006.
- Of the estimated United States child population in 2006, approximately 10.8 million were African American.
- African American children made up approximately 14.7% of the Unites States child population (under 18 years) in 2006.

Child Maltreatment

- During 2006, an estimated 905,000 children were determined to be victims of child maltreatment (abuse or neglect) by this nation's child protective services (CPS) systems. Approximately 22.8% of these child maltreatment victims were African American.
- The approximate distribution of African American child maltreatment victims by type of maltreatment is as follows: 51.9% were victims of neglect; 12.9% were victims of physical abuse; 5.5% were victims of sexual abuse; 1.4% were victims of medical neglect.

Children Entering Foster Care

- Approximately 295,000 children entered the US foster care system in FY 2006.
- Of the children entering foster care in 2006, approximately 27% were African American.
- Approximately 79,000 African American children entered the US foster care system in the in FY 2006.
- African American children entered foster care at a rate 1.8 times their presence in the US child population.
- African American children were approximately 2.4 times more likely than white children to enter the US foster care system in 2006.

Children Exiting Foster Care

- Approximately 279, 000 children exiting the US foster care system in FY 2006.
- Of the children exiting foster care, approximately 28% were African American.
- Approximately 76,600 African American children exited the US foster care system in FY 2006.

Children In Foster Care (Out-of-Home Care)

- Approximately 493,000 children were in the US foster care system at the end of FY 2006.
- Of the children in the US foster care system in 2006, approximately 33% were African American.

- Approximately 161,000 African American children were in the US foster care system at the end of FY 2006.
- African American children were present in the US foster care system at a rate 2.2 times their presence in the US child population.
- African American children were 3.2 times more likely to be in the US foster care system than white children in FY 2006.

Children Adopted from Foster Care

- Approximately 50,700 children were adopted from the US foster care system in FY 2006.
- Of the children adopted from the US foster care system, approximately 27% were African American.
- Approximately 13,800 African American children were adopted from the US foster care system in FY 2006.
- In 2006, African American children were 2.4 times more likely than white children in to experience adoption from the US foster care system.

Children Waiting to be Adopted from Foster Care

- Approximately 138,000 children were waiting to be adopted from the US foster care system at the end of FY 2006.
- Of the children waiting to be adopted, approximately 32% were African American.
- Approximately 44,000 African American children were still waiting to be adopted from foster care at the end of FY 2006.

- African American children were 3.3 times more likely than white children to be waiting for adoption from the US foster care system.

Data Sources

- Child Welfare League of America. (2008). Special tabulation of the Adoption and Foster Care Analysis Reporting System. Washington, DC: Author. Accessed on April 2, 2010.
- U.S. Department of Health and Human Services, Administration on Children, Youth and Families. *Child Maltreatment 2006* (Washington, DC: U.S. Government Printing Office, 2008).

- Note: Disproportionality and disparity-related calculations performed by Oronde A. Miller using the above data sources. This fact sheet is available on the Institute's website at www.ifcwb.org.

About the Institute for Family and Child Well-Being

www.ifcwb.org

IFCWB MISSION

Founded by Oronde Miller in January 2004, and guided by the collective experience and wisdom of our National Advisory Council, The Institute is committed to telling the story of African American children and families that have been affected by both the American child welfare and juvenile justice systems. We are primarily a comprehensive information resource center for information about African American children, families and communities, as well as their historical and contemporary experiences with the American child welfare and juvenile justice systems. It is our intent to collect, develop and provide the information necessary to fundamentally transform the way this nation understands and addresses matters related to child and family well-being, especially with respect to African American children, families and communities.

The mission of The Institute for Family and Child Well-Being is to: a) make accessible culturally meaningful information about the experiences of African American children and families involved in this nation's child welfare, juvenile justice and related systems, including relevant challenges; and b) provide information and assistance to professionals and organizations involved in providing direct services and/or administering programs for African American children and families involved in this nation's child welfare, juvenile justice and related systems. It is our hope that in doing this work we will also increase the capacity of African American families and communities to provide for and protect our children.

Much of the Institute's work is designed to support our online resource repository (www.ifcwb.org). This website is managed by Oronde Miller, the Institute's Founder and Executive Director, with the guidance and support of the Institute's National Advisory Council.

IFCWB CONCEPTUAL FRAMEWORK

Guiding Principles

Employment of a Strengths-Based Perspective

African American families have identifiable strengths, including those articulated by Dr. Robert Hill in *The Strengths of Black Families.* These strengths include, among others: a) an achievement orientation; b) a work orientation; c) flexible family roles; d) kinship bonds; and e) a religious orientation. Professionals working with African American families must be committed to identifying these strengths, and utilizing them to frame any additional assistance and support that may be needed.

An Appreciation of Culture and Tradition

The practices of the African American extended family system are rooted in the historical and cultural value systems of our African ancestors, passed on from generation to generation and for centuries before and after our arrival in "the Americas." Just as communities and families change, so do the expressions of a community's culture, tradition and values change over time. It is expected that individuals and organizations working most effectively within the African American community and with African American families should be able to recognize and appreciate the nuances and expressions of African American culture, its traditions, values, etc., and incorporate this perspective into their work.

Ethic of Collective Responsibility for Ensuring the Well-Being of Families and Children

African American families and communities have historically assumed responsibility for the care, protection and nurturance of its children. African American life in contemporary American society has significantly impacted the traditional forms of expression of this ethic of shared and collective responsibility for ensuring the well-being of families and children. While the expression of this ethic may have been significantly impacted as a function of living and adjusting/coping within contemporary American society, it is still present in the African American extended family system and support networks. It is expected that individuals and organizations working most effectively with African American families and communities should be able to recognize and tap into this support system in an effort to effectively meet the needs of the families and children in their care.

Appreciation of Informal Adoption as a Natural Response... Implications for Kinship Care, Subsidized Guardianship and Other Placement Options

The majority of African American children who find themselves unable to live with their biological parents continue to be cared for and provided for within this "informal" extended family / kinship system. This has been a characteristic of African American family life for centuries. Individuals and organizations working with African American families must recognize the fundamental discomfort among many African Americans with the notion of "Termination of Parental Rights." Consistent with this, many African American families are reluctant to formally adopt relatives via the American legal system given the fundamental challenges/contradictions presented by formal adoption to pre-existing family roles and relationships within many African American families and communities. Child welfare professionals and policy-makers must be mindful of these dynamics when considering the policy and resource implications of kinship care and subsidized guardianship, (as well as other possible temporary and longer-term placement options for children).

Context of Child Welfare System Involvement

Enhancing a Community's Capacity to Ensure Family and Child Well-Being / Investment in Prevention Efforts

It is imperative that child welfare systems invest more resources into family preservation efforts, including the provision of more intensive home-based services and supports necessary to keep families intact. Public child welfare agencies, however, should not carry the full responsibility of providing direct services and supports to families in need. There are community based organizations that do this work well. Unfortunately, they are too often under-funded, under-resourced, and have limited organizational capacity. It should be a goal of public child welfare agencies to assist these smaller, yet effective, organizations in developing the organizational capacity needed to most effectively meet the needs of greater numbers of families. This would be a worthwhile investment of resources in support of improved family and child well-being outcomes.

Minimal Level of Agency Intrusion

Removal of children from their immediate families should be the option of last resort. The majority of African American children who come to the attention of the child welfare system do so because of an allegation of some form of neglect, rather than physical and/or sexual abuse. On the other hand, the majority of White families that come to the attention of the child welfare system do so because of an allegation of abuse. When these allegations of abuse and neglect are substantiated, African American families are more likely to be separated while white families are more likely to be provided in-home services. African American families must also be provided effective in-home services and supports to keep the family intact, while increasing their capacity to meet the material needs of their children.

Priority Placement Consideration for Relatives and Extended Family Support Network

When it is determined that a child must be removed from her or his immediate family, every effort must be made to place the child with a relative or some other member of the extended family support network. Such placement options are more likely to minimize the trauma experienced by both the child and her or his parents during the period of separation. This approach requires agencies to do a better job of identifying potential relative support and placement resources, as well as other members of the family's extended support network at the very earliest stages of a family's involvement with the child welfare system.

Reunification as First and Preferred Permanency Goal

As soon as it is appropriate and safe, children must be reunified with their families of origin. Many professionals agree that children grow up best in a family setting that is familiar to them and with family members that are committed to and invested in their longer term healthy growth and development. Much of the data suggests that public child welfare agencies, in general, do *not* do a better job providing for and ensuring the safety of children in their care in comparison to the childrens' families of origin. Interestingly, when children do age out of foster care (often upon reaching their eighteenth or twenty-first birthday) they almost always go right back home or to a relative. These are often extremely unstable living arrangements, however, suggesting these very children should really be considered homeless. It only makes sense that public child welfare systems invest the resources necessary to support a more formal reunification plan that enhances the likelihood of a successful transition back into the family.

Alternative Permanency Considerations for Children and Families

When family preservation efforts fail, agencies must act promptly to place children in other more suitable "permanent" homes. As mentioned previously, initial consideration should be given to relatives and other members of the extended family support network. These placements should be given the same support resources and subsidies afforded non-relative placement resources. Recent research suggests that kinship care and subsidized guardianship placements produce similar and better outcomes for children than traditional foster care and "stranger" adoption placements. It is incumbent on public child welfare agencies to seek out the most suitable placement options for children in need of permanency, even when it takes more time or requires flexibility in waiving non-safety-related requirements.

Long-Term Impact of Child Welfare System Intervention on African American Children, Families and Communities... Individual and Collective Impact

The general public tends to be more aware of the immediate impact of child welfare system involvement on the children and immediate families directly involved in the intervention efforts of public child welfare systems. What has not been explored nearly as much is the collective impact of child welfare system involvement on the broader network of family and community members connected to families directly experiencing child welfare system intervention, as well as the African American community-at-large. In her book, *Shattered Bonds*, Dorothy Roberts began to explore the broader social and political impact of punitive child welfare system intervention on the African American community. This is a line of work and investigation in need of greater exploration and discussion.

Long-Term Support for Children, Families and Communities Impacted by Child Welfare System Intervention

Involvement with this nation's public child welfare system is often a very traumatic experience for children and families. Involvement with child protective services can easily last for the greater part of a year or more for a family. Compounding this experience is the reality that previous involvement with the child welfare system increases the likelihood of future involvement. This cycle has a long-term impact on the children, families and communities involved. For children and families experiencing more punitive child welfare system intervention this experience produces even greater long term effects. Public child welfare systems must be more responsive in providing the longer term support and resources needed by families that have been impacted by their work and intervention efforts.

FIVE MAJOR CHALLENGES

1. A State of Crisis Exists... Our Stories Must Be Told

There is a state of crisis within the African American community, particularly as it relates to the involvement of so many of our children and families with this nation's child welfare and juvenile justice systems. The greater African American community must be made aware of this crisis, and must be engaged in the identification and implementation of solutions. The goal is not only to improve the outcomes of African American interaction with the child welfare and juvenile justice systems in this country; the goal must be to increase the capacity *and will* within the African American community to be agents of change, healing and community development. Other individuals and organizations involved in this work must be respectful of and responsive to African American leadership of this work.

Social scientists and researchers have, collectively and historically, done an inadequate job of describing and discussing the complexities and the integrity of the African American experience in this country, particularly as it relates to child development and family functioning. The stories of African American families and children invlolved with this nation's child welfare and juvenile justice systems must be told. These stories can best be told by the individuals that have actually lived and/or been impacted by the experience.

IFCWB Commitment: The Institute for Family and Child Well-Being will: (a) participate directly in the documentation and sharing of these stories; (b) support community institutions, researchers and other social scientists in their attempts to effectively document and share these stories; and (c) work with key individuals and organizations to clarify and execute an agenda to shape the national discussion about the meaning and implications of these experiences to the present and the future of African American families and communities.

2. **Racial Disproportionality and Disparate Outcomes is Both a Societal and Institutional Injustice**

African American children have been and continue to be disproportionately represented in this nation's foster care *and* juvenile justice systems. African American children are represented in each of these systems in numbers far greater than their proportion of the population. African American children and families also receive disparate treatment by, and services from, this nation's child welfare and juvenile justice systems. African American families must have access to the services and support resources that enhance their ability to provide for, nurture and protect their children. The current reality (as well as the historical conditions that have created it) represents a grave injustice that the African American community and American society-at-large must work deliberately and quickly to rectify.

IFCWB Commitment: The Institute for Family and Child Well-Being will actively spread the word about these dynamics and their impact on both individuals and the community-at-large, as well as work directly with key individuals and institutions to more effectively mobilize the African American community and contributing systems into informed and strategic action.

3. The construct of Race has historically defined, and continues to define, the fundamental nature of African American child, family and community interactions with institutional structures in American society.

African American families are more likely than their White counterparts to be reported to child protective services for suspected abuse or neglect (even with similar presenting circumstances), are more likely to have their children removed from their care, and receive fewer and less timely services to assist in resolving any underlying challenges they may be experiencing. When African American children do enter care, they are more likely to be placed in congregate / group care settings, stay in foster care longer, and receive fewer reunification-related or permanency-related supports and services than their White counterparts.

These dynamics highlight the reality that race largely influences the service delivery and decision making processes of this nation's child welfare systems. A thorough examination of the role of structural, institutional and individual level racism is imperative for individuals and organizations concerned about and/or involved in this work.

IFCWB Commitment: The Institute for Family and Child Well-Being will work closely with key individuals and organizations to further explore and document the effects of individual, institutional and structural racism on African American families and communities. We will also work to undo these effects, while promoting the healing and continued development of African American families and communities.

4. Culturally Centered Practice is an Imperative

There is a tremendous need for more effective and culturally centered methods of supporting African American families while strengthening their capacity to provide for and protect their children. Similarly effective approaches to the education and training of child welfare professionals must also be identified and/or developed, then shared with others around this country. There are likely many effective models and approaches already in existence. These models and approaches must be identified, better understood and shared with others around the country.

IFCWB Commitment: The Institute for Family and Child Well-Being will work with other key individuals and organizations to develop, document and share effective culturally responsive and affirming strategies for meeting the real needs of African American families and communities.

5. Easy Access to Accurate and Reliable Information is Needed

Legislators and child welfare policy makers do not seem to have access to the most accurate and/or complete body of information regarding African American children, families and communities, particularly as it relates to: a) dynamics of child abuse and neglect, b) decision making dynamics in the foster care and juvenile justice systems, c) access to relevant and responsive child / family support services, d) access to affordable health care, e) access to affordable housing, f) access to jobs that provide a livable income, and g) adequate access to culturally responsive substance abuse and mental health treatment and services. There is obviously a great need for a central and independently operated repository of information about the experiences of African American families in this country, especially the experiences of African American children and families involved with this nation's child welfare and juvenile justice systems.

IFCWB Commitment: The Institute for Family and Child Well-Being will use its website and online information and resource repository (www.ifcwb.org) to provide easy and reliable access to related information and resources. We will continue to partner with interested individuals and institutions to make this site as responsive as possible to the needs and interests of its users.

The Institute for Family and Child Well-Being was created to support the field in responding to these major challenges. With the support of our National Advisory Council as well as our network of concerned professionals and community members around this country, we stand ready to support professionals, organizations and communities in meeting these challenges.

A NOTE ABOUT THE AUTHOR

Oronde Miller is the Founder and Executive Director of the *Institute for Family and Child Well-Being*, and has served as a Senior Director of Strategic Consulting for Casey Family Programs; Senior Research Assistant at the Child Welfare League of America; and as Research Associate for the National Center on Permanency for African American Children.

An educator and psychologist by training, Oronde has a particular interest in family dynamics, schooling and education, and the reclamation of traditional African methods of character formation and development among children and adolescents.

Oronde and his brother briefly experienced foster care as young children, before being adopted and raised in a wonderful African American family in Detroit, Michigan.

Oronde currently lives in Prince Georges County, Maryland, just outside of Washington, DC.

LaVergne, TN USA
20 September 2010
197797LV00002B/1/P

9 780982 484012